Charlotte M. Wilson
ANARCHIST ESSAYS

ANARCHIST CLASSICS

Charlotte M. Wilson
ANARCHIST ESSAYS

edited by Nicolas Walter

FREEDOM PRESS
LONDON

Charlotte M. Wilson (1854 - 1944)
Anarchist Essays (1884 - 1900)

This collection edited by Nicolas Walter and
published in 2000 by Freedom Press
Angel Alley, 84B Whitechapel High Street
London E1 7QX

© 2000 Freedom Press & Nicolas Walter.

ISBN 0 900384 99 9

Cover design by Clifford Harper
Typeset by Jayne Clementson

Printed in Great Britain by Aldgate Press
Units 5/6 Gunthorpe Workshops, Gunthorpe Street, London E1 7RQ

Contents

Introduction

CHARLOTTE M. WILSON was the best-known of the small group of middle-class intellectuals who played an important part in the emergence of the British anarchist movement during the 1880s. In particular she was the main founder and the first editor and publisher of *Freedom*, the long-standing voice of mainstream anarchism in Britain, and the leading figure in the Freedom Group during the first decade of its existence.

*   *   *

Charlotte Mary Martin came from a professional family. She was born on 6 May 1854 at Kemerton, a village near Tewkesbury on the Gloucestershire-Worcestershire border. She was the only child of Robert Spencer Martin, a doctor and surgeon from a prominent local family, and of his wife Clementina Susannah Davies, from a prosperous commercial and clerical family. She received the best education then available to girls, going to Cheltenham Ladies' College (where she was very unhappy) and then to Cambridge University (where she was very happy). From 1873 to 1874 she attended the new institution at Merton Hall which later became Newnham College (not, as has often been said, Girton College); she took the Higher Local Examination (roughly equivalent to the later GCE Advanced Level) at a time when women couldn't take university examinations or degrees at Cambridge. While at the university she lost her religious faith and moved towards the political left.

Two years after leaving Cambridge, in 1876, she married Arthur Wilson (a distant cousin, who was born in 1847, went to Wadham College, Oxford, and became a stockbroker in 1872). They lived first in Hampstead, where she was active in charitable and educational work. After a process of political development which remains obscure, they both adopted increasingly progressive views. At the end of 1885 they adopted the fashionable 'simple life' by moving to Wyldes, an old cottage in what was then open country at North End on the edge of Hampstead Heath, and she refused to live on her husband's earnings. She took part in the Society of Friends of Russian Freedom, which was inspired by the Russian revolutionary exile Stepniak (Sergei Kravchinski), and in the Men and Women's Club, which was organised to arrange frank discussion of sexual problems by the social scientist Karl Pearson (her many letters to him are preserved in the Pearson Papers held at University College, London). But above all she took part in the Socialist and Anarchist movements. One of the elements in her political development was the mass trial of Anarchists at Lyon in January 1883, at which Peter Kropotkin and dozens of French comrades were sent to prison, and which was widely reported in the British press. During the following year she became a public advocate of both Socialism and Anarchism.

*   *   *

Charlotte Wilson's first known public political action was a letter about women workers which appeared in March 1884 in *Justice*, the paper of the Democratic Federation, which had been formed in 1881; in August 1884 it adopted a Socialist policy and became the Social Democratic Federation, which she joined. In October 1884 she also joined the Fabian Society; this had been founded as the Fellowship of the New Life by a group of progressive intellectuals in 1883, but became the Fabian Society in January 1884, with a more or less Socialist programme. She was the only woman elected to its second executive in January 1885. Her fellow members included such people as Annie Besant, Hubert Bland, Havelock Ellis, Sydney Olivier, Bernard Shaw, Graham Wallas, and Sidney Webb, and she had no difficulty in holding her own with them. In the later memoirs of early Fabians, she is remembered mainly as a hostess, like Edith Nesbit, but she was in fact a leading member of the society for a couple of years. Also in October 1884 she formed a study group which met at her house to read and discuss the writings of Continental Socialists such as Marx and Proudhon (which were not then available in English) and the history of the international labour movement, and which provided much of the early philosophical and factual background for the lectures and pamphlets which became the main Fabian contribution to Socialist propaganda.

Her particular contribution was to inspire an Anarchist fraction within the Fabian Society. As Shaw put it with his customary exaggeration in the first of his unreliable histories of the Fabians, when she joined "a sort of influenza of Anarchism soon spread through the Society" (*The Fabian Society: What It Has Done and How It Has Done It*, 1892). In fact the fraction didn't have much influence, and it didn't last long, but for a time it was significant. On 7 November 1884 she read a paper on Anarchism, which was the basis of four articles published during November and December 1884 in *Justice* signed 'An English Anarchist'. This was one of the first English-language expositions of Anarchist communism at a time when none of the relevant writings had yet appeared in English. As she wrote to Karl Pearson, "my paper was not the development of a private theory of my own. It was simply an attempt to summarise in English dress the views of a party which exists in every country in Europe, and counts many hundreds of thousands of adherents" (19 December 1884). A little earlier she had given him an eloquent summary of her idealistic version of Anarchism:

> It is because Anarchism abjures altogether a cut-&-dried reorganisation, because it reconciles the modern passion for absolute personal freedom with the growing desire for social unity that it seems to some of us an ideal worth fighting for. All its hopes for the future are based upon spread of a higher morality & in making an uncompromising war upon the principle of arbitrary authority in all its forms, it only seeks to destroy what stands directly in the way of moral progress. (30 October 1884)

In 1885 she helped to start and was closely involved with the first explicitly Anarchist paper published in Britain, *The Anarchist*, which was edited and published by Henry Seymour from March 1885. She got Bernard Shaw to write for its first issue his famous article on anarchism ('Give a Dog a Bad Name: As an Anarchist Might Put It') – which he told Seymour "was written more to shew Mrs Wilson my idea of the line an anarchist paper should take in England than as an expression of my own opinions" (letter, 5 January 1885), and which was immediately printed in Benjamin Tucker's anarchist paper *Liberty* (11 April 1885) as his first publication in the United States. She contributed money and material to it for more than a year, and she became the leading member of the 'English Anarchist Circle' which was formed around it. During 1885 she wrote two well-informed articles about the French Anarchist movement and two particularly interesting articles on the general subject of Justice and on the particular issue of the new Criminal Law Amendment Act.

During 1886 she produced three further essays on Anarchism – 'Social Democracy and Anarchism', another talk given to the Fabian Society during 1885 and published in the first issue of *The Practical Socialist*, the short-lived monthly paper of the Fabian Society; 'The Principles and Aims of Anarchists', a talk given to the London Dialectical Society in June 1886 and published in one of the last issues of *The Present Day*, a short-lived secularist paper; and a pamphlet called *What Socialism is*, a Fabian Tract. This last consisted of two parts – a section on 'Collectivism' (i.e. state socialism), which Friedrich Engels was invited but declined to write and which was instead written anonymously by Charlotte Wilson, and a section on 'Anarchism' (i.e. non-state socialism) which was written and signed by Charlotte Wilson – preceded by an anonymous introduction, also written by Charlotte Wilson.

Charlotte Wilson's expositions of Anarchism were necessarily rather repetitive, as she tried to say fairly similar things to slightly different audiences, and inevitably rather derivative, as she translated into English terminology the Anarchist Communism which had already been developed on the Continent, especially by Peter Kropotkin and Elisée Reclus. She fully accepted the prevailing view that the class struggle – between 'monopolists' and 'workers', in her vocabulary – was the basis of Socialism, that Anarchism was a form of Socialism, based on the abolition of property as well as of authority, and that violence, however undesirable as a general principle, was inevitable as an occasional practice in the coming social revolution. At the same time she insisted that Anarchism was also a development of Liberalism, and she tried to domesticate it for her British audience by deriving it from such acceptable writers as John Stuart Mill and Herbert Spencer.

In all this she made no claim to originality, but only to expressing the views of her fellow Anarchists in Britain. In fact it isn't clear how far she really did speak for the growing Anarchist movement. She doesn't seem to have had much contact with the working-class militants in the growing trade unions and socialist organisations. Henry Seymour, a former Secularist who had become an Anarchist Individualist, with whom she collaborated for a few months, discounted her contact with anyone. When she attended a Fabian Congress in June 1886 as a representative of the 'London Anarchist Group of Freedom', he suggested that she probably did so only in the sense that she had written her contribution to the Fabian pamphlet "on behalf of the London Anarchists"; and he commented: "Unfortunately she admitted in my presence that she wrote on her own behalf only, and without consulting the London Anarchists at all."

But she was certainly the leader of the Anarchists in the Fabian Society. On 17 September 1886 the Society organised a meeting at Anderton's Hotel in Fleet Street, where representatives of the various Socialist organisations in London debated the question of forming an orthodox political party on the Continental model. A motion to this effect was proposed by Annie Besant (the former colleague of Charles Bradlaugh in the National Secular Society, and later successor of Madame Blavatsky in the Theosophical Society) and seconded by Hubert Bland (husband of Edith Nesbit):

> That it is advisable that Socialists should organise themselves as a political party, for the purpose of transferring to the hands of the whole working community full control over the soil and the means of production as well as over the production and distribution of wealth.

William Morris (the leading member of the Socialist League, and the best-known Socialist in Britain) proposed and Charlotte Wilson was one of those who seconded a dissenting rider:

> But whereas the first duty of Socialists is to educate people to understand what their present position is, and what their future might be, and to keep the principles of Socialism steadily before them, and whereas no Parliamentary party can exist without compromise and concession, which would hinder that education and obscure those principles it would be a false step for Socialists to attempt to take part in the Parliamentary contest.

The parliamentarians defeated the anti-parliamentarians by a two-to-one majority (27 - 40 for the rider, 47 - 19 for the resolution), and the Fabians society – and the bulk of the British socialist movement – was set on the course which it has followed ever since. (According to the Fabian Society minutes, "Subsequently to this meeting the Secretary received notice from the Manager of Anderton's Hotel that the Society could not be accommodated there for any future meetings"; according to an added note by Shaw, "This was because one Graham, a tinsmith and an Anarchist follower of Morris, came drunk and comported himself with unseemly heat"!)

The Fabian Society formed the Fabian Parliamentary League in February 1887, and Charlotte Wilson left the Executive Committee in April 1887. She didn't take a leading part in the society for two decades, though she maintained her membership and continued to take part in its social activities.

*   *   *

By that time she had anyway committed herself entirely to the Anarchist movement. She corresponded with Kropotkin's wife while he was in prison in France, and when he was released in January 1886 he soon settled in England, partly as the result of an invitation from her group. For a time they continued to work with Henry Seymour, and the April and May issues of *The Anarchist* were produced under "conjoint editorship" as a journal of Anarchist Communism. But the experiment failed, the group parted from Seymour, *The Anarchist* reverted to individualism in June, and he published his attack on her in July. Relying on Kropotkin's cooperation and prestige, and on Wilson's contacts and ability, the group decided to start a new Anarchist paper on the model of Kropotkin's own paper *Le Révolté* (which began in Geneva in 1879, moved to Paris in 1885, and as *La Révolte* and then *Les Temps Nouveaux* remained the leading French Anarchist paper until the First World War).

The first issue of the monthly *Freedom* was dated October 1886, though it was actually published in time for the Anderton's meeting (Shaw noted buying a copy there in his diary), and the Freedom Group eventually became the Freedom Press, which for more than a century has remained the main publisher of Anarchist literature in Britain. The most prominent person involved was of course Kropotkin himself, but Charlotte Wilson was the organiser of the group, the editor and publisher of the paper, and also its main supporter and contributor. She was normally responsible for the editorial article in each issue – such as the eloquent article on 'Freedom' which opened the first issue – and also for most of the political and international notes. She contributed only a few signed articles, signing herself austerely as 'C.M.W.' or 'C. M. Wilson'; the most important of these was a series on 'The Revolt of the English Workers in the XIX Century' (June-September 1889). During her editorship she attracted a remarkable group of contributors, including Edward Carpenter, Havelock Ellis, Edith Nesbit, Henry Nevinson, Sydney Olivier, Bernard Shaw and Ethel Voynich, as well as many obscure but devoted Anarchists from several countries. She was also involved in establishing Anarchist discussion meetings in London and encouraging local groups outside, and for a few years she was an active lecturer and debater at various kinds of meetings all over the country. As well as *Freedom* itself, she helped to produce a series of Freedom Pamphlets from 1889 onwards, editing and translating some of them, and writing one herself – *Anarchism and Outrage* (1893), a reprint of a leading article she had written about the Anarchist view of violence.

In January 1889 *Freedom* was temporarily suspended because of her illness, and when it was resumed in March 1889 it was edited by James Blackwell with the help of "a committee of workmen". When Blackwell left, she took over again in February 1891 and continued for another four years, with occasional gaps because of illness, when Nannie Dryhurst deputised for her. In January 1895 *Freedom* was again temporarily suspended again because of illness in her family. This time she resigned permanently as both editor and publisher, and when the paper was again resumed, in May 1895, it was edited by Alfred Marsh, who continued until his death two decades later. Although she was a great admirer of William Morris, she felt unable to contribute to the tributes written after his death in 1896. She ceased to take an active part in the group, though she kept in touch and continued to contribute money and material for a few years. In particular, in 1896 she produced the draft for 'A Brief History of *Freedom*', an anonymous account of the paper's beginnings. In a covering letter to Marsh (28 September 1896), she wrote:

> It is strange to look back all these years & recall the things that seemed so all important then & that one has forgotten now, worries, & difficulties & seeming impossibilities all passed through & left behind & the details fading out of recollection, but a certain rich result remaining in actual fact from the work we all did together.

When it was eventually published, in 1900, Marsh added only a few words at the beginning and end of her draft and also omitted most of the details of the various contributors she had named.

* * *

Charlotte Wilson took no part in left-wing politics for a decade, during which both her parents died, and her main public activity was in the campaign for the preservation of Hampstead Heath as a public open space. During this period she wrote *Wyldes: A history* (1904), the story of her house. When she did resume political activity, she returned not to the Anarchists but to the Fabians. In 1905 the Wilsons moved to St John's Wood in London, and in 1906 she became involved in the Society again.

During the rise of the militant campaign for women's suffrage, she joined several feminist organisations – The Women's Industrial Council, the Women's Local Government Society, the Women's Freedom League – and in 1908 she took the lead in forming the Fabian Women's Group. This met at her home, and she was its founding secretary and most energetic member from March 1908 until she resigned because of illness in December 1915. The group did much research and campaigning work for women, and Edith Morley described her as "the fount and inspiration" of it in *Women Workers in Seven Professions* (1914). She herself described its activities in *Fabian Women's Group: Three Years' Work, 1908-1911* (1911). She was again a member of the Fabian executive from 1911 until 1914. She also joined the Independent Labour Party and several other parliamentarian organisations. In 1912 she recalled her past, when she organised the public celebration by liberal intellectuals of the 70th birthday of her old comrade, Peter Kropotkin.

During the First World War she left politics altogether. By then the Wilsons had settled in the country near Reading. At the end of the First World War she was honorary secretary of the Prisoner of War Fund of the Oxford & Buckinghamshire Regiment, and in 1919 she was appointed an officer of the new Order of the British Empire for her services to the welfare of prisoners of war. She seems to have taken no further part in political activity. Arthur Wilson died in 1932, and she was looked after until her death by their distant cousin, Gerald Hankin. They went to the United States, and she ended her life in a home, suffering from senile dementia, and dying there at Irvington-on-Hudson on 28 April 1944, a few days before her ninetieth birthday.

*   *   *

Charlotte Wilson was for a decade the best-known native Anarchist in Britain. Her work as a writer and speaker was distinguished by inspiration, intelligence and industry, reticence, reliability and respectability. She always remained very much an intellectual, and very much in the background. She steered her way between the militants and the moderates in the Anarchist movement, but she was definitely a Communist rather than an Individualist, and she later moved from revolutionary to parliamentary Socialism. It is notable that when she concentrated on Anarchism she showed little interest in Feminism and that when she concentrated on Feminism she showed little interest in Anarchism. It is also notable that she won the friendship of all who worked with her and the respect of all who knew her. Her particular contribution to *Freedom* and the Freedom Press was to set them up and to set them on their way as a serious paper and publisher with a solid basis, providing a model which they have tried to follow ever since.

She has been little more than mentioned by historians of the British left – usually inaccurately – but for a few years she was a familiar figure. She was frequently reported in the Socialist and Liberal press at the time, and she was frequently remembered in subsequent memoirs of the period. Socialists tended to be hostile but respectful, but Liberals tended to be patronising as well. A good example is an anonymous report of her contribution to the meeting at South Place commemorating the Paris Commune on 17 March 1887:

> ... a slender person, bordering on middle age, but on the right side of the border, dressed becomingly in black, and with hair trained forward in an ordered mass to form a sort of frame of jet for a thin, thoughtful face. The type is the South Kensington or British Museum art-student, the aesthete with 'views', and Mrs Wilson quite realised it as to the views. She was decidedly anarchical ... What she did say was delivered with great clearness of enunciation, with great purity of accent, with a certain appearance of effort, not to say of fatigue, as though the hall taxed her voice beyond its powers, and with the monotonous calm that is perhaps the most common outward sign of the born fanatic. She was quite womanly and lady-like to use the good old-fashioned word ... (*Daily News*, 18 March 1887)

She also became the model for characters in several political novels. The best-known of these is Gemma in *The Gadfly* (1897), a romantic evocation by her friend Ethel Voynich (née Ethel Boole) of the Italian Risorgimento, in which she is an Englishwoman living in Italy who is small and dark, quiet and calm, and the heart and soul of a Republican group in Florence; but the book says nothing interesting about her true character. (Incidentally, the occasional claim that Charlotte Wilson was the lover of Kropotkin seems to be derived from recollections of Ethel Voynich in old age.) A more direct but very brief portrait appears in *A Girl Among the Anarchists* (1903), a satirical evocation by 'Isobel Meredith' (the pseudonym of Helen and Olivia Rossetti) of the bomb era of the early 1890s, in which the authors were personally involved. Charlotte Wilson is introduced as Mrs Trevillian, "an aesthetic, fascinating little lady"; but she plays no part in the plot, and again nothing is said about her character.

The most striking portrait appears in *The Anarchists* (1891), an ideological "Picture of Civilisation at the Close of the Nineteenth Century" by John

Henry Mackay, a German-Scottish follower of Max Stirner, who had been active in London as an Anarchist Communist during the 1880s. The autobiographical hero Auban describes the various tendencies and personalities in the movement, and includes in his account of the meeting of 14 October 1887 at South Place protesting against the impending execution of the Chicago Anarchists the following description of Charlotte Wilson:

> Beside the table on the platform was standing a little women dressed in black. Beneath her brow which was half hidden as by a wreath by her thick, short-cropped hair, shone a pair of black eyes beaming with enthusiasm. The white ruffle and the simple, almost monk-like, long, undulating garment, seemed to belong to another century. A few only in the meeting seemed to know her; but whoever knew her, knew also that she was the most faithful, the most diligent, and the most impassioned champion of Communism in England ... She was not a captivating speaker, but her voice had that iron ring of unalterable conviction and honesty which often moves the listener more powerfully than the most brilliant eloquence.

More than a century later, that epitaph may stand unchanged.

*   *   *

Charlotte Wilson's life has been generally neglected. Passing references to her appear in letters, memoirs or biographies of several of her contemporaries, and inaccurate descriptions of her in accounts of the Fabian Society and of British anarchism by several historians. There is an unpublished biography by Hermia Oliver, and an academic thesis by Susan Hinely – *Charlotte Wilson: Anarchist, Fabian, and Feminist* (Stanford University, 1987). See also '*Freedom*: People and Places' (*Freedom: A Hundred Years*, October 1986), 'Notes on *Freedom* and the Freedom Press, 1886-1928' (*The Raven* 1, April 1987), and 'Charlotte M. Wilson, 1854-1944' (*The Raven* 21, January/March 1993). There will be an entry on her in the *New Dictionary of National Biography*.

Charlotte Wilson's writings have been generally neglected. Her article on the Criminal Law Amendment Act was immediately published in a slightly revised form as a pamphlet. Fabian Tract number 4 was never reprinted, but her own contribution was reprinted as the first Free Commune pamphlet in 1900 and in *Freedom* in December 1907, and it has occasionally been reprinted by the anarchist press since then. All three 1886 essays on anarchism were reprinted in a pamphlet as *Three Essays on Anarchism* (Cienfuegos Press 1979, pirated by Drowned Rat 1985). *Anarchism and Outrage* was reprinted in 1909, and was included in *What is Anarchism? an Introduction* (1993). The present collection of her writings on Anarchism includes these four items, together with the four articles from *Justice*, the two articles from *The Anarchist*, the whole of *What Socialism Is*, the leading article in the first issue of *Freedom*, later articles on work and on Democracy and Anarchism, and the complete version of 'A Short History of *Freedom*'. The texts have been reproduced from the original versions with only minimal corrections of obvious misprints and misspellings.

Nicolas Walter

Acknowledgements

Thanks are due to: Bishopsgate Institute, London; British Library, London; British Library of Political & Economic Science, London School of Economics & Political Science (Fabian Society Papers, G. Bernard Shaw Diaries, and marked set of *Freedom*); Freedom Press, London; International Institute of Social History, Amsterdam (Freedom and Socialist League Collections); Newnham College, Cambridge (information about C.M. Martin); University College, London (Karl Pearson Papers); and to Heiner Becker, Susannah Brunert, Stuart Christie, Hermia Oliver, Christine Walter, and Fred Woodworth.

Anarchism

An English Anarchist

I

The word Anarchism is open to such grievous misconstruction from English readers, who associate it with mere confusion, or, still more unfortunately, with acts of personal violence and revenge, that, in the absence of any more competent co-religionist at liberty for the moment to undertake the task, I would crave your permission to explain what our creed really is and especially its bearing on social reconstruction.

Anarchy, as your readers are aware, means simply "without a ruler" or "chief magistrate". Anarchist, therefore, is the name assumed by a certain school of Socialists, who, in the words of the Declaration of the Forty-Seven at Lyons, believe that "the time has come to teach the people to do without government", as well as for teaching them the advantages of common property. They believe that, in the present stage of progress, social union can only be stable when it is based upon absolute economic equality, and perfect individual freedom. They further believe that the rottenness and injustice of the present constitution of society is reaching a climax, and that a revolution is inevitable which shall sweep away privilege, monopoly and authority, with the laws and institutions which support them, and set free the constructive energies of the new social ideal already growing up within the outworn formulas of a past phase of civilisation.

Their conception of the mission of revolution as purely destructive, leads Anarchists to face the query of the unknown future less in the form of – What scheme have we to substitute for the status quo? than – *After the annihilation of the oppressive institutions of the present, what social forces and social conditions will remain, and how are they likely to be modified and developed?*

It is hardly needful to inquire, as some cavillers are fond of doing, what would happen if civilised men ceased to be social animals and existed each for himself alone. We do not live together in societies and mutually yield and accommodate ourselves to one another so as to make a common existence possible, because we are coerced to do so by certain laws and institutions. We are drawn together by our social instincts, and moulded into such harmony as we have at present attained, by the perpetual action and reaction of the influence we exert over each other, and by our inherited and acquired habits, sympathies, and beliefs. The Revolution, in breaking up the stereotyped forms into which some of these social instincts and beliefs have crystallised, can, in no sense, destroy the social instincts themselves.

Since the ordered and systematised society of mediaeval Europe was dissolved by Individualism, these social instincts have made themselves most powerfully felt in the growth of two vast and ever increasing forces, i.e., Socialised Production and Public Opinion. Both are the direct outcome of the influence of personal freedom, and the energy of individual initiative upon the action of society. Both are amongst the realities, which Revolution directed against shams and hypocrisy, will leave unscathed.

The present highly socialised system of production on a large scale, with its endless division and sub-division of labour, its machinery, its concentrated masses of human "hands", and its complex industrial relations, has taught men the enormously increased command over the forces of nature, which they may obtain by co-operating for existence. It is, moreover, already practically a system whereby all workers labour for society as a whole, and, in return, supply their needs from the general stock of finished products. When the individual monopoly in land and capital which prevents the workers, firstly, from directing their own labour and, secondly, from adequately supplying their wants, is destroyed the end of social reconstruction must be to enable them to do both as simply and effectually as possible. Will free co-operation and free contract enable the workers to carry on production on a scale adequate to their needs, if they retain the necessary instruments in their own hands, without any State or Communal organisation and direction to take the place of monopolists, masters and organisers? We believe that they will. For a radical change must have come over opinion as to the nature of property and public duty before the Revolution can succeed. Proudhon's famous dictum, "*Property is theft*", is the key to the equally famous enigma proposed to Socialists by Saint-Simon, when he wrote, "*From each according to his capacity, to each according to his needs*". When the workers clearly understand that in taking possession of railways and ships, mines and fields, farm buildings and factories, raw material and machinery, and all else they need for their labour, they are claiming the right to use freely for the benefit of society, what social labour has created, or utilised in the past, and that, in return for their work, they have a just right to take from the finished product whatever they personally require, the difficulty will be solved and obstacles in the shape of making necessary changes in the detailed working of the system of production and its relation to consumption, will vanish before the ingenuity of the myriad minds vitally concerned in overcoming them. But until they do realise, that, as long as land and capital are unappropriated, the workers are free, and that, when these have a master, the workers also are slaves, no lasting and effectual improvement can be wrought in their condition. The fatal passion of acquisitiveness has got such hold upon men's minds, that masterless things appear now to many of them as monstrous an anomaly as masterless men did to the country justices of Queen Elizabeth. They devise all sorts of elaborate schemes for putting the common property of the people in trust, and appointing administrators to direct its application – a masterful sort of servants, likely to become worse tyrants than the old ones. We Anarchists, who desire neither to rule nor to serve, prefer to trust to the reason of the workers, enlightened by their bitter experience of past slavery.

Anarchism proposes, therefore, – 1. That the usufruct of instruments of production – land included – should be free to all workers, or groups of workers. 2. That the workers should group themselves, and arrange their work as their reason and inclination prompt (including those who manage the means of communication). 3. That the necessary connections between the various industries and branches of trade, should be managed on the same voluntary principle, and that the task of furnishing intelligence as to the relations of production and consumption (by means, for instance, of the public press, special trade journals, offices for information, &c.), should be left to brain workers, whose taste leads them to make industry a special duty. 4. That finished goods should be massed in large stores and markets, and that offices for facilitating the mutual convenience of producers and consumers (as for example, house builders and carpenters, and house seekers) should be opened in convenient centres. 5. That each individual should supply his needs therefrom as his self-knowledge prompts.

This is the theory of *laissez faire*, modified and extended to meet the needs of the future, and avoid the injustice of the past. It implies that the majority of men are capable of acting with some approximation to effectiveness, if left free to do so, and is based on the assumption that the individual is the best judge of his own capabilities, and, further, that self-interest, intelligently followed, tends to promote the general economic well-being of the community. It differs from the old system in placing self-interest on the side of just distribution, by the destruction of private property in the means of production, and thus does much to neutralise the dangers of Society from natures whose selfishness is their strongest sentiment. It also allows free play to those social sympathies, the influence of which in determining conduct it was one of the chief mistakes of the orthodox economists to ignore. It assumes that just and generous economic relations are for the interest of the individual, and that he is capable of being taught so, if not by science and the teaching of the moralist, then by the stern lessons of experience. Has not the process of instruction already begun?

[*Justice*, Volume 1, Number 43, 8 November 1884]

II

The economic theory of Anarchism puts an end to no competition but that for a share of the produce. It affords facilities for the perpetual change and variation on which progress depends. It leaves untouched the influence of emulation, and puts no check upon individual initiative and individual enterprise, upon the friction of opposing methods and ideas, the stimulating irritation produced by contrasted idiosyncrasies and tastes, and the energy inspired by single-handed struggle with difficulty. It gives free scope to the fresh interest, the exercise of originality, and the artist's delight in producing, which make work a pleasure, when, and when only, it is the result of free, spontaneous impulse. But Anarchism unites with the dignity of self-directed labour, the joy of known and recognised endeavour in a common cause, the thrill of a conscious part in the common life, that social spirit which drudgery has driven out of our wage-slaves, even whilst their actual interdependence has increased.

"The struggle of men to outvie one another in production is beneficial to the community; their struggle over the joint produce is not," says Arnold Toynbee. It is commonly, however, asserted that it is necessary to make men work, unless some authority take its place; and we are accused of imagining that we can secure the advantages of competition without its evils, by destroying the mainspring on which its action depends. If the only motive for work is the desire for material wealth, how can the immense amount of voluntary labour, and the frequent choice of the (personally) less productive kinds of labour which we actually see at the present day, be accounted for? Men work from a variety of motives – a desire for fame or honour, the love of invention, the pleasure of creating, or of merely exercising their faculties of mind and body, and giving vent to their energy, and last, but not least, they work for the gratification of doing something useful to others. These are no exceptional sentiments and desires – some of them, at all events, are visible in all children. When their cultivation becomes of paramount importance to the community it will surely not be neglected. Looking at the question from another point of view, let us ask if it is really necessary for a man of average intelligence actually himself to feel the pangs of hunger before he can realise that his labour is essential to the life of the community, and consequently to his own. We believe not. We believe that the vast majority of men are capable of understanding the necessity of work, and that therefore the pressure of public opinion will bear so heavily as to be unendurable upon the idle members of the future society; consequently a very much smaller number will be idle than now, when privileged idleness is looked upon as no disgrace.

It may be objected, that though most men may be willing to work, it does not necessarily follow that their work will be of social utility. But in the great majority of cases habit and education have prepared workmen for nothing but taking a small and definite share in a huge system of production, whether they be sufficiently intelligent to estimate the advantages of such a system or no. When, after the Revolution, existing wealth is consumed, and the workers find themselves face to face with the imperative necessity of working to supply their needs, the method of working to which they will turn will naturally be that to which they are accustomed. It is equally certain, however, that, when they find themselves their own masters, they will modify the old system to suit their convenience in a variety of ways, e.g., short hours for each, supplemented by a succession of shifts to save cost of production, remodelled workshops, factories, &c., with regard to comfort and safety; discontinuance of the manufacture of useless luxuries; improvement of the quality of articles of universal utility; the application of machinery to saving labour of the disagreeable sort (as this sort of work will probably, at first, be left to the most intelligent of the community, the development of invention in this direction is likely to be very rapid), and such other changes as common sense is likely to suggest to free men.

One other objection must be glanced at. Co-operation, it may be urged, has not hitherto been eminently successful. Is not that amply accounted for by the extent to which it has been hampered by the conditions and prejudices of existing society with regard to (a) capital (b) remuneration? The first is obvious; not so the second. Co-operative societies in professing to abandon competition amongst themselves for the fruits of their joint labour, still retain the fallacious belief that in the present system of production it is possible to award to each worker the exact proportional social value of his labour. Amid endless jealousies and heart-burnings they attempt to substitute an arbitrary division according to some fixed rule or theory of utility for competition. This root of bitterness is destroyed by the Anarchist theory of distribution.

Does Anarchism, then, it may be asked, acknowledge no *meum* or *tuum*, no personal property? In a society in which every man is free to take what he requires, it is hardly conceivable that personal necessaries and conveniences will not be appropriated, and difficult to imagine why they should not. Anarchism contemplates no hard and fast line between common and personal belongings, any such individual arrangements and mutual concessions are easily conceivable when there is plenty for all. When property is protected by no legal enactments, backed by armed force, and is unable to buy personal service, its resuscitation on such a scale as to be dangerous to society is little to be dreaded. The amount appropriated by each individual, and the manner of his appropriation, must be left to his own conscience, and the pressure exercised upon him by the moral sense and distinct interests of his neighbours.

[*Justice*, Volume 1, Number 45, 22 November 1884]

III

I endeavoured in my last letter to explain the Anarchist theory of economic development and its relation to the existing system of production. It remains to consider the social and political aspects of Anarchism and its bearing upon present tendencies and ideas.

It passes as a truism, that public opinion – the expression of the collective moral sense – is the real sovereign of to-day. Its sanction has replaced the old religious sanctions as a moral restraint. Law is supposed but to give voice to its mandates, and deliberative assemblies to be its humble servants. It is admitted, that the voice is muffled and unintelligible, and that the servants are treacherous and remarkably ineffective; but it is supposed that Democracy can change all that by judicious lopping and enlargement. In that supposition we Anarchists do not agree. We believe – not only what all thinkers already admit, that a large proportion of the misery of mankind is attributable to bad Government – but that Government is in itself essentially bad, a clumsy makeshift for the rule of each man by his own reason and conscience, which, in the present stage of civilisation, has served its turn.

The idea of government sprang in barbarous times from the authority of the leader in war, and the patriarchal rule of the head of the family; it grew up in the superstition born of the fears of an ignorant age; and on the brute instincts and childishness, the ignorance and fears of mankind it has prospered ever since, until progress began slowly and surely to cut away the ground under its feet.

Whilst government was viewed as a divinely appointed arbiter in the affairs of the uninspired commonalty, it was naturally deemed its duty to watch over its subjects in all their relations, and provide, not only for their protection from all force or fraud but its own, but for their eternal welfare. But now that government and law are looked on as mere conveniences, forms destitute of sanctity, and possessing no authority but such as the aggregate of the nation are pleased to allow, it may be worth considering, if the collective life of the community cannot find expression in some fashion less costly in time, wealth, and human freedom. The future of Democracy in England, as depicted by the *Pall Mall Gazette* for August 11, is not very re-assuring to any but ambitious politicians. "The time in fact, is already upon us, when there is no vital difference between parties, only an unscrupulous scramble for place." If Liberals, however, strike out in a new direction, and accept the policy of opposition to the powers of Parliament, vindicated by Mr Herbert Spencer, they can hardly fail to reduce the authority of representative government to so thin a semblance that true Liberty will be plainly visible behind it, and Liberalism be forced by a logical necessity into Anarchism. For representation – the middle-class panacea for all ills, now on its trial – recognises in theory the right of each individual to govern himself, whilst at the same moment it forces him to delegate that right to a representative, and, in return, bestows the privilege of a practical claim to tyrannise over every one else. The freedom of the collectivity to crush the individual is not, however, true Liberty in the eyes of Anarchists. It is one of those shams, which the Revolution is to destroy.

We believe, opinion to be the real and inevitable expression of collective existence in civilised communities, and that its natural outlets in the public press, in literature and art, in societies, meetings, voluntary combinations of all sorts, and social intercourse are amply sufficient to enable it to act as a binding and corrective force in a society relieved from privilege and private property. Even now it is the strongest deterrent from crime; even now its punishment is the bitterest, its reward the highest, and its rule of conduct the most absolute for the average mortal. Yet, unfortunately, its sense of right and wrong is continually blunted and falsified by the action of the authorised exponent of justice. At the present day law is supposed in the abstract to represent the moral sense of the community as against its immoral members. Practically it cannot do so. Public morality is continually fluctuating and, by changing as fast as its want of dignity will admit, law cannot keep up with it and only succeeds in stereotyping the mistakes from which opinion is just shaking itself free, and fitting old precedents upon new conditions, where naturally they look absurd, and do mischief. Being framed to suit a variety of cases, no two of which are alike, it is actually unjust in every one, moreover, becomes so complicated, that after all the efforts of a specially trained class to expound it, its awards are uncertain and mysterious to all concerned. The modes of punishment are necessarily brutal and degrading, not only to those who suffer, but to those who inflict them, and its attempts to enforce contracts and settle disputes, cause at least as much suffering as they avert. Law stands and – from what experts say of the difficulties of reform – must ever stand, hopelessly in the way of morality, rendering a higher conception of it impossible to the mass of mankind, and consequently to the public opinion, which represents them.

[*Justice*, Volume 1, Number 46, 29 November 1884]

IV

When the collective moral sense is relieved of the incubus of law, it may still be unjust in many instances, but its injustice will take a less permanent form and one more capable of rectification, whereas its sense of justice may be perpetually widened and increased by the growth of knowledge and human sympathy. Certainly, judging from its present influence, it will be strong enough to serve as a restraint upon those individuals, who refuse to respect the rights of others. But when Society has ceased deliberately to condemn certain of its members to infamy and despair from their birth, there are both physical and moral grounds for the belief that the "criminal classes" will cease to exist. Crime will become sufficiently rare to give the mass of the population courage to face the fact that moral depravity like madness, is a terrible affliction, a disease to be carefully treated and remedied, not punished and augmented by ill-treatment. We know this now, but we are too cowardly or too Pharisaical to admit it.

Prevention, however, is better than cure, and the surest mode of securing virtuous citizens, as well as healthy public opinion, is by a sound system of education. The rough discipline of the Revolution will clear the air of many prejudices, and serve to raise men's minds to a higher conception of justice and of duty, but it is on the training of children that the future of society mainly depends. I wish I could quote the fine passages in which Michael Bakounine outlines the Anarchist theory of education in his *Dieu et l'Etat*, but that would be trespassing too far upon your space. Suffice it to say, that Anarchism considers that the one end and aim of education is to fit children for freedom. Therefore it teaches, firstly, that intellectual training should be scientific, cultivating the reason and leading it to understand and recognise the immutability of the laws of nature, and to conform to them in all things, taking knowledge of them for rule and guide in place of the arbitrary enactments of men; and, secondly, that moral training, starting with the necessary absolute authority, should proceed by the gradual removal of restraints, and by the inculcation of personal dignity and responsibility, respect for others, and the worship of truth and justice for their own sake, to form free men and women filled with reverence and love for the freedom of their fellows. This view of the subject is familiar also to readers of Mr Herbert Spencer.

The creed of Anarchism is the cultus of Liberty, not for itself, but for what it renders possible. Authority, as exercised by men over their fellows, it holds accursed, depraving those who rule and those who submit, and blocking the path of human progress. Liberty indeed is not all, but it is the foundation of all that is good and noble, it is essential to that many-sided advance of man's nature, expanding in numberless and ever-conflicting directions, which Walt Whitman likens to the weather, where "an infinite number of currents and forces, and contributions and temperatures, and cross purposes, whose ceaseless play of counterpart upon counterpart brings constant restoration and vitality". For is not the tendency of all rules and organisations to stiffen into set shapes, destitute of life and meaning, one of the chief causes of social deterioration?

Viewed in relation to the thought waves of our times, the strength of Anarchism seems to us to lie in its full recognition and acceptance of two lines of thought, which, though their respective champions delight to pose them as in hopeless conflict, are uniting to bring about the social revolution, i.e., Individualism and Socialism. It ignores neither the splendid triumphs of Individualism in thought and action, nor the need for brotherly association, which Mazzini considered years ago as the primary necessity of modern Europe; but it holds that the longing for freedom, and the growing sense of the dependence of each on all, the responsibility of all for each, are advancing side by side, and that one cannot be sacrificed to the other without provoking a violent re-action. Therefore do Anarchists oppose all measures which tend to increase the power and influence of governments, even if their immediate result seems to be an improvement in the condition of the people. Anarchism is a new faith, as yet imperfectly formulated, and it has been met in the society of privilege with such bitter persecution, that it has retorted with the violence of despair. Contemned, hunted down, reviled, calumniated even in death, the existence of an Anarchist on the Continent at this moment is scarcely more endurable than that of a Christian in the days of the Roman Empire, victim like himself of the hatred of the world for an enthusiasm of humanity beyond its comprehension. But from other Socialists at least, Anarchists should meet with the fair recognition and justice, which you, Sir, have shown in allowing the publication of these letters.

[*Justice*, Volume 1, Number 47, 6 December 1884]

Justice

An English Anarchist

On the wind-swept brow of a Surrey hill, commanding on every side one of the loveliest of English landscapes, lies a desolate mound, where, according to vengeful local tradition, the bones of malefactors were burnt as they fell, a disjointed heap, from the gibbet hard by. But where that gibbet stood, where one cruel tooth iron still projects from its ancient stone supports, the gentler feeling of a later time has erected an obelisk with the inscription, *In tenebris lux; in luce spes.* A fit emblem of the change which is slowly creeping over the attitude of society towards the most miserable of its members. For them indeed has arisen a light in the darkness, and in the light there is hope.

Once all the sympathy of humane men was reserved for the victim of wrong. Now that the influence of conditions, physical and social, in determining character and action, and the limits which these conditions impose on individual responsibility, are better understood, we bestow at least equal pity upon the wrong-doer. And with pity comes the fellow-feeling which teaches us how near we, each one of us, stand to the criminal. Circumstances have perhaps developed our nature in a different and, it is to be hoped, a more social direction, or we have inherited a stronger will, a larger brain, or better physique, or as is most probable, a happier fate has left us unembarrassed by the difficulties and temptations which have led him astray. But beneath all difference of outward seeming the likeness of nature still remains, and the sense of brotherhood lies deeper than the sense of divergence and repulsion. The current morality of mere form and respectability has encouraged us to repress this natural feeling, but as men grow more truly social it forces its way to the surface, and suggests the reflection, "If my brother or my dearest friend had been overtaken in such a fault, how would all the best impulses of my nature prompt that he should be dealt with? Could I honestly and from the bottom of my heart acquiesce in hanging or penal servitude or imprisonment as the best possible means of reclaiming him? Is this sort of arbitrary punishment the suffering that quickens and warns; the kind of pain which nature inflicts on unfitness for her conditions? Is it, in a word, the natural and inevitable result of my friend's unsocial qualities and likely to check them and develop those more suited to social life?" You would not desire to spare him, even if you could, the natural consequences of his fault. The disgust, the avoidance, the distrust of his fellows; his own self-reproach and remorse. He must learn by experience that wilful injury to others is incompatible with personal happiness, when men are living in a social condition. But do you think that he will ever learn that in jail? He is more likely to learn to hate his fellow-men and to come out only to avenge himself for the wrong they have done him. They have revenged themselves upon him, and now he will have his turn. So we get a "criminal class" with no other occupation than to prey upon and injure their neighbours.

The Nineteenth Century owes a debt of gratitude to Victor Hugo for the powerful and pathetic expression he has given to this rising feeling of human sympathy with the pariahs of our civilisation. Lawyers and critics may scoff at idle sentimentality as they list, but no one who has read the story of Jean Valjean, or *The Last Days of a Condemned Man*, can again be indifferent to the crimes committed by Society against its criminals in the sacred name of Equity.

"Revenge," said Lord Bacon, "is a sort of wild justice." It will be our aim in future numbers to show, all official disclaimers and professions of fine moral sentiment to the contrary, that justice as now administered is nothing better than a sanctimonious and hypocritical form of revenge.

[*The Anarchist*, Volume 1, Number 5, July 1885]

The Criminal Law Amendment Act

An English Anarchist

"It would be better done to learn that the law must needs be frivolous which goes to restrain things, uncertainly and yet equally working to good and to evil. And were I the chooser, a dram of well-doing should be preferred before many times as much the forcible hindrance of evil-doing." Thus wrote John Milton 241 years ago in his plea for free printing, and never has the principle for which he so eloquently contended stood in more need of vigorous expression than it does to-day. The Criminal Law Amendment Act is a case in point. Our Society, starting terrified from the spectacle of its own corruption, hastens to clap a plaster, in the form of an Act of Parliament, upon the sore which offends its sight. The remedy is so easy that men do not stop to enquire if it is likely to be effectual. "Legislation to render impossible the recurrence of such enormities" is a phrase which will act as lullaby to the conscience of many a well-meaning Englishman. The Act will become law; the demonstration in Hyde Park will, in the language of Mr Stead, pronounce a more or less noisy "damn"; and then the agitation will die away, as others have done before, to be succeeded by some newer sensation or merged in the excitement of the General Election.

There has been a great talk during the last few weeks about the necessity for courageously scrutinising all the ghastly details laid bare by the Pall Mall Commission; perhaps it may be at least equally necessary to summon courage to face the causes from which such horrors spring.

There are two closely entwined causes which lie near the root of the whole matter. One is the economic condition which we have allowed to grow up amongst us, and which we are now maintaining by all the powers of the State. We have allowed property in land and moveables to be *monopolised*. Wealth acquired by force or fraud, or by exploiting the labour of others has become the personal private property of individuals, who have no just claim to it, since it is not of their creation. Nevertheless these monopolists have secured their possession by the laws which they have manufactured to defend themselves, and we all tamely look on and submit. The result is that the monopolists own all the means and materials for work, and the rest of the nation, the large majority, are in a sense their

slaves. That is to say, that those who have no share in the monopoly of
property must work that they may live, and they can only work on the
terms the owners of land and capital choose to impose. These terms are
the sale of their power to labor, of their intelligence and their muscles, for
so many hours a day, at such wages as will keep as many of them alive and
in working condition as the capitalists and landlords want. Our boasted
English liberty is for the worker merely the liberty to sell himself on the
best terms he can obtain, and to force his way into the class of
monopolists, if good luck, penuriousness, and sharpness enable him to do
so. Under these conditions the lion's share of the social wealth produced
by the joint labors of the industrious members of the community continues
to pass into the hands of the monopolists, who are consequently enabled
to live in idleness and spend their time and energy in that effort to find an
outlet for their wasted powers which they call amusing themselves. Their
existence is a fevered search for new sensations; and those in whom the
animal nature is strongly developed are led by satiety into brutal excesses,
which it is hardly possible for a healthy mind to conceive, and which are
as much a result of a diseased mental and physical condition as
Nebuchadnezzar's desire to eat grass. Such abominations have reappeared
in every society founded on servile relations between man and man as the
crisis of its fate drew near. They are the natural fruit of every form of
slavery. The rich, having taken advantage of the necessities of the poor to
buy their labor-force, and make them work for their profit, easily to go on
to buy their bodies to minister to their pleasures. Civilised existence is a
great market where the buyer, the seller and the commodity is man. What
wonder if some of the wage-slaves copy and pander to the vices of their
masters, and the pollution spreads through all ranks of society. What
wonder if starving women sell themselves and one another and their own
children into the lowest depths of human degradation.

Thus we are brought face to face with the deeper moral cause, which lies
at the bottom of these evils as of every sort of oppression and wrong, the
cause of which our disgraceful economic relations are but one outcome. I
mean that barbarous contempt for human nature, which is the basis of all
self-degradation and of all unsocial feeling and conduct, and the hot-bed
not only of mere animalism but of all conceptions of life which can
properly be called materialistic. It took shape formerly in the scorn of the
privileged individual for the vile herd. In modern thought it re-appears in
the callous disregard of the mystical entity Society for the individual man.
Any cruelty, any outrage upon human dignity is justified, if only it can be

represented as making for the preservation of Society. The mental, moral and physical degradation of unfortunate women is described by one historian of the development of the new fetish, as the price Society must pay for the purity of home life. Society pays the price with heroic indifference. The value of the purity gained we have lately learned. In such a moral atmosphere self-respect withers, and with it the sense of individual, personal responsibility, and of reverent regard for the rights of every individual man and woman, the growth of which is the essential condition of all social union worth the name. The consequences are visible in such abominable measures as the C.D. Acts on the one hand, and the brutalities recorded by the *Pall Mall* on the other.

How does this new imposition of restraints by the clique who are pleased to consider themselves as representing Society, propose to deal with the two causes we have named?

One of the principal objects of the Criminal Law Amendment Act is to put a stop to the *sale* of children under sixteen, but it ignores altogether the economic conditions which produce such sales. Even a middle-class organ like the *Daily Telegraph* admits, "Not wickedness but want underlies nine-tenths of the profligacy of London, and if we could remove competition and misery, we should abate sin more effectually than by any amount of inexperienced outcry or penal laws." But the grievance is not that our legislators leave absolutely untouched the conditions which condemn thousands and hundreds of thousands of children to ruin. They are well-advised not to attempt the absurdity of trying to alter economic relations by Act of Parliament. The wrong they do is to persist in still maintaining our present unsatisfactory relations by force, because they dare not for one instant face the consequences to their self-interest, or as they would prefer to put it, the consequences to Society, of freeing social wealth from the artificial protection of law.

The Bill, therefore, confines itself to morals, and endeavours to protect individual rights by making girls under sixteen wards of the government, and by visiting outrage by fraud or violence with various penalties. Let us concede that possibly it may conduce to the punishment of a few vicious persons and save certain other persons from injury. But even so the questions still remain – what are the corresponding evils of such legislation, and is it the best means of raising the standard of that respect for human nature which is the mainspring of virtue?

Now this Act of Parliament places the power of irreparably injuring the character and prospects of innocent men, into the hands, firstly, of rash and meddling philanthropists, who if they always act honestly, most assuredly do not always act wisely or with complete knowledge; secondly of the class who, as they have sold themselves, cannot be expected to be scrupulous about trading upon others; thirdly of the victims of hysteria or of a morbidly vicious organisation; fourthly of little children, in whose minds the relations between sensation and consciousness are frequently so imperfectly developed that they are incapable of distinguishing truth and falsehood, and who, moreover, are completely under the sway of older and possibly worthless people. In many such cases it is impossible to obtain the direct evidence of more than one witness and that witness the plaintiff. And the delicate task of solving these difficult problems is left to the infallible British juryman, whose competence in matters appealing to his sentiment and his prejudices was so happily illustrated in the condemnation of the guiltless Mr Hatch to five years' penal servitude for a crime of this nature, which existed only in the imagination of two naughty little girls. Thus whilst the Bill aims at preventing fraud and intimidation in one direction, it opens a wide door for both in another. It has left undefined the meaning of the "false representations" for which it imposes a penalty; it renders it dangerous for a man to offer a fainting woman a glass of sherry unless in the presence of witnesses; but, to take one example of fatuity out of many, it leaves unchecked the very common cruelty of enticing young girls into disorderly houses as servants. After several despairing attempts to frame a clause to meet this evil, Honourable Members decided that after all the case was provided for, because if a little maid asked any lady who might offer to engage her, if she (the lady) were the keeper of such an establishment and afterwards found the answer given to be false, the girl could prosecute her mistress!

But inadequacy and temptation to intimidation and fraud are not all. It is only necessary to allude to the clauses (1st) giving power to a court of law to take any girl from her parents or guardians and hand her over to anyone it thinks fit, if it imagines there is reason to believe that the parents or guardians are responsible for the girl's degradation, and (2nd) permitting anyone who can persuade a magistrate at any hour of the day or night that he or she is a person having a *bona fide* interest in a young woman, to thereupon obtain a warrant to enter any house with the police, and forcibly carry off the said young woman, – it is only necessary to allude to these clauses to suggest the wrong and suffering within their power to inflict in the hands of foolish or unscrupulous meddlers and stupid or indifferent officials. In the debate on this Act itself, a member stated that he *knew* of one magistrate who derived part of his income from houses let for immoral purposes. The police and the rulers of society have been shown to be so largely implicated in the evils complained of, that it is surely the most arrant folly to entrust them with the remedy.

Already, before the Bill has become law, some of those who have the subject at heart are marking their sense of its certain insufficiency. They remember that the information which has horrified England, lay for four years unheeded in the Blue Books, until public opinion took the field by means of a newspaper agitation. Vigilance Committees, Purity Societies, voluntary associations of all sorts, the Hyde Park Demonstration itself are so many tributes to the uselessness of law-making and law-makers. "This is not a matter in which man or woman can save the state by deputy," so writes even the *Pall Mall Gazette*, "We must do it ourselves, or it will not be done." In the days of Wat Tyler, before the spirit of Englishmen had been ground down by capitalist slavery and submission to law, men knew how to defend their daughters' honour without whining for the protection of an Act of Parliament. According to the statements of Mr S. Smith in the House of Commons, this is still the case in young and healthy communities. There crimes of the sort so inadequately prevented by this Bill are always punished by lynch law; and for the miserable wretches who live by betraying their fellow-creatures, and the victims of loathsome and unnatural desires such discipline is the greatest kindness. It supplies the severe physical shock which is their best chance of recovery from their diseased condition. Whereas the artificial substitute of imprisonment, as Michael Davitt has shown in his *Prison Recollections*, only forces the morbid mind to feed upon itself, and affords it opportunity to spread its corruption.

In short, the feeble and vicious enactment known as that for the Amendment of Criminal Law is the worthy output of a nation whose manhood is in abeyance, of a community which pins its faith to majority rule, and expects to be made virtuous *en bloc* by a perfected system of representation. It deals neither with the economic nor the moral causes of vice, and the best that can be hoped for it is that it may remain practically a dead letter, like most of its predecessors in the trivial task of patching together a moribund society. As for us, who share Milton's creed, and believe in the strength of good to cast out evil and of life to overcome death our hopes are fixed upon the dawn of that change in thought, word and deed which is beginning to be known amongst men as the social Revolution.

APPENDIX

For those, who, like ourselves, are already striving towards the emancipation of mankind from exploitation and authority, but stung by a burning sense of shame for the guilt of the community of which we form part, long to take immediate and active steps to purify its atmosphere from the foulest of taints, we add a few suggestions as to remedies which seem to us worth trying.

1. EDUCATION – The equal and common education of boys and girls. Physiological instruction to take the place of the ignorance and mystery which breed morbid curiosity and lead to the problem of sex relations and the origin of life assuming unhealthy proportions in the mind. Special training for girls in independence of thought, and courage in action and in acts of self-defence, to counteract the cowardice and weakness engendered in women by ages of suppression and slavery.

2. MARRIAGE – (a) Open acceptance of the truth that parenthood as a result of marriage is a matter of distinct choice, and ought only to be undertaken by those who wish for the responsibility. (b) Non-intervention of the State in marriage relations. Consequent removal of the social stigma unjustly attaching to free unions which are the result of mutual affection and respect, and the transfer of social contempt to *property* marriages which are mere legalised prostitution.

3. SOCIAL INTERCOURSE – Contempt for all conventional restraints preventing free and open friendship between men and women and hinder true knowledge of one another's character, views, and feelings. Formation of associations for such communication. One such Club has already been started in London.

4. PROTECTION – Training Homes and Technical Schools to teach girls to gain their living independently. Also where they may take refuge when out of employment. Women's Trade Unions.

5. DEFENCE – Opposition to the contemptuous tone often adopted by men toward women, and prompt resistance in word, and if need be, in deed against every insult offered them, however slight. Immediate chastisement of offenders without reference to the police, quibbles, uncertainty, and delay of a law-court. Boycotting and denunciation of all shops and employers on whose premises vice is deliberately encouraged or is rendered inevitable by starvation wages.

[*The Anarchist* (Volume 1, Number 6, 15 August 1885); *The Criminal Law Amendment Act*, 1885]

Social Democracy and Anarchism

C.M. Wilson

It has not yet been recognised in England that the Socialism which is being put forward throughout the civilised world as a remedy for the acknowledged evils of modern society – wears two distinct faces. When it is said that a man is a Socialist, it is implied that he regards the monopoly of private property in the means of production as the cause of the existing unequal distribution of wealth and its attendant ills; but the philosophical grounds of his belief, and his practical deductions from them remain indefinite as ever. Putting aside those so-called Socialists, who only aim at reforming our present social arrangements so as to relieve, for the moment, the misery, without an attempt to fathom either its ultimate cause, or its ultimate issue; Socialists are divided into the centralising and decentralising parties, the party of the State and the party of the federatic commune, and this political difference is the outward sign of a grave difference of principle.

It is needless to dwell here at great length upon the beliefs of the Socialists of the State, the Social Democrats: their views are already familiar to the English Public through the publications of the Social Democratic Federation.

Roughly speaking they may be summed up as follows: – Man, is the creature of his conditions. His moral, social, and political state at any given time is exactly what his economic circumstances have made it. Human progress means increasing ability to derive from Nature the largest amount of subsistence with the smallest expenditure of energy, and the discovery of the best social arrangements for the distribution of what is so obtained. The problem now before us, is, how to modify the external conditions of human existence so as to secure to all men the most complete enjoyment. The means for working it out, lie ready to our hands. Misery has resulted from individual monopoly of the means of production, let us therefore, transfer land and capital to the State. The State, as it is now, is the engine of class rule; it can only reflect the economic phase through which we are passing. True Democracy – the government of the people by themselves – can only advance hand in hand with Socialism. The advance of the people to political power will serve us

as a lever to bring about their economic salvation. We can make use of the
organised force of the State as it is to transform the machinery of
Government into that, and the State as it ought to be. The main business
of society, organised for self-government, should be the regulation of the
business of production and exchange in such a manner that each citizen
shall be obliged to perform his fair share of social labour and receive in
return a corresponding share of social produce.

Thus men are to be freed from wrong and oppression by the alteration of
their external conditions, and their external conditions must be altered by
organised force: i.e., by seizing upon the State as it is. To obtain a hold on
the State we must enter in political arena and use political methods:
political methods in a democracy mean the art of obtaining command over
the strength of numbers, and these numbers must be won by an appeal that
the masses can understand. The lofty ideal of the socialised State appeals
to the moral sense of the thoughtful few: but to the ignorant masses in their
bitter need, must be preached the gospel of hate and spoliation. The people
supply both the dynamic force and the raw material essential to eager
social reconstructors, and so each one scrambles for a place in the popular
favour that he may have opportunities to work out his scheme in his own
way. As in other political conflicts – other things being equal – the man
who wins is he with the loudest voice, the readiest flow of words, the
quickest wit and the most self-assertive personality. Immediately it
becomes the business of the minor personalities to drag him down, and the
old struggle for place and power repeats itself within the very socialistic
societies themselves. There is authority on one side and revolt on the
other, and the very forms which are supposed to be the safeguards of
liberty are made engines of personal enmities.

Social democracy in every land is thus setting out for the new Jerusalem,
along the same old muddy political tracks, of which some of us are so
weary, and the Holy City to which it aspires, is to be built up of the old
bricks and mortar of property and authority: but the bricks are to be set the
other way up and refaced so as to look smart from the outside. In
economics, in the renunciation of the individual monopoly of capital,
social democracy belongs to the future; but in politics, in its conception of
the community organised administratively, it belongs to the past.

The history of men living in a social state is one long record of a never-
ending contest between certain opposing natural impulses developed by
the life in common. The slow development, the contest between these
opposing instincts, within each man, has repeated itself within each society.

As the one set of impulses or the other have triumphed in the individual man or woman, he or she has sided with one party or other in the community. But in the vast majority of cases no definite triumph has been won: the man or woman has been swayed hither and thither between social and anti-social desires, without conscious realisation of their nature. Looked at for short periods the life of society seems to bear the same impress of fluctuation and uncertainty, but regarded as a whole, it becomes distinctly apparent that the slow course of evolution is tending to eliminate the one sort of impulse and to develop the other into increasing activity.

The struggle of which we are beginning to be dimly conscious within our own nature and in the world of men around us, is that between the anti-social desire to monopolise and dominate, and the social desires which find their highest expression in fraternity – the equal brotherhood of men. This distinction is not equivalent to that often drawn between altruism and egoism, between the self-regarding impulses and those which regulate our relations with our fellows – neither is it another mode of expressing the difference in human relations commonly expressed in the words selfish and unselfish. A selfish man may find it more for his own ease and interest not to attempt to dominate or monopolise, and an unselfish man may be honestly convinced that it is his painful duty to rule his neighbours for their own good.

The desire to dominate is the desire to make oneself superior to one's fellows, to be distinguished from them or placed above them by some acknowledgement of superiority. It is the desire to take and keep whatever may conduce to one's own superiority or importance. The social impulses and desires summed up in "fraternity" are the reverse of all this. They prompt the wish to be on terms of equal companionship with our fellow-men, to share with them all gifts of nature or circumstances, to exchange ideas or opinions on their own merits, and to decide on common action by mutual agreement and sufferance.

The increasing consciousness of self which marks our age, is revealing to us more clearly these opposing currents of desire, both in ourselves and others. We are often keenly aware within ourselves of a desire to rule some fellow-creature, who tempts us by his servility or his feeble defiance: of a sense of equal social relationship towards another who meets us on a ground of equality and equal self-respect; or of an instinct of self-defence called out by the aggressive personality of a third. It is this personal experience which is leading us to a clearer conception of the true meaning of the strife we see around us.

The battle is for freedom, for the deliverance of the spirit of each one of us, and of humanity as a whole, from the government of man by man; whether such coercion justify itself on the plea of superior strength or superior wisdom, of divine light or necessity, of utility or expedience; whether it take the form of force or fraud, of exacted conformity to an arbitrary moral code, or an arbitrary social system, of the open robbery of the means of subsistence, or the legal appropriation of the universal birthright of land, and the fruit of social labour.

This freedom is the necessary preliminary to any true and equal human association, and until this is recognised in theory as the basis of human relationship, state social union is impossible.

Anarchism is the conscious recognition of this naked truth. It stands face to face with the spirit of greed and domination, and declares a moral compromise out of the question. In the light of past victories, won upon many a changing and ill-defined battle-ground, it confronts the enemy of to-day in the latest of his protean shapes, and demands the destruction of the monopoly of property, and of its guardian – the law. Slavery and serfdom are past, political despotism is shrinking away towards the East, and constitutional monarchy is withering before our eyes. Wage slavery and class supremacy is doomed, and our Bourgeois Parliaments are on the high road to talk themselves out of existence, but property and law are still hedged about by that divinity which has ceased to smile on kings.

Property is the *domination* of an individual, or a coalition of individuals, over things; it is not the claim of any person or persons to the use of things – this is, usufruct, a very different matter. Property means the monopoly of wealth, the right to prevent others using it, whether the owner needs it or not. Usufruct implies the claim to the use of such wealth as supplies the user's needs. If any individual shuts off a portion of it (which he is not using, and does not need for his own use) from his fellows, he is defrauding the whole community.* The only claims which any member of a community can fairly put forward to a share of the social wealth are 1st. That he requires it to develop and maintain in efficiency all his faculties and powers. 2nd. That he has contributed towards the production of that wealth to the best of his ability. 3rd. That (as regards any particular article) he has put so much of his personal labour into it as to have a prior claim

---

* Property – in the sense understood by the Proudhon School – may perhaps be defined as wealth controlled by one who does not use it except to make an engine of extortion against someone who does use it. In this sense a field let by a landlord is his property, but a similar field cultivated by the owner is his possession – EDITOR.

to its first use. The first claim is a part of that larger claim that each individual has upon the social feeling of the community of which he is a member; the claim that he shall – as far as the means of the community will admit – have space and opportunity for the fullest development of which his nature is capable. What is required for such development only the individual himself can judge, it varies in every particular instance. But not only is such opportunity pleaded for by the social feelings of such of us as believe the highest development to lead to the highest happiness, but it is urged by the self-interest of the community; for the best developed members of a community are certainly the most useful to it as a whole. It is the highly developed who feel most strongly that healthy desire for the exercise of their faculties which leads to the doing of the best and most earnest work, and this is the most effectual stimulant to exertion. That stimulant which is afforded by the desire to appropriate as much wealth as possible from the general produce – is not only inferior to intensity but it leads a man to choose – not that work which is most useful or for which he has most natural appetite, but rather such work as pays best: a choice which naturally results in "scamping" and inferior workmanship. The utilitarian arguments for the monopoly of property would not suffice to uphold it against the sense of justice which has grown up in humanity, were it not for the guardianship of law. Law encircles private property with some of its own sanctity – a sanctity arising from the fact that it is supposed to represent – in some mysterious manner – that which is in the abstract eternally right. "Thou shalt not steal" as embodied in the statute book is supposed to afford a special sanction to monopolists in possession, however their wealth may have been come by, or is used.

"This reverence has a foundation, in fact, there is a certain small kernel of written law that does represent the social code of habits, customary and desirable in daily life, habits the utility of which has commended itself to the common moral sense of mankind, as a rough generalisation from experience. But men have forgotten that the conditions to which that experience applies vary slightly in each individual case, and in each succeeding generation. To have this social morality – written and fixed is an obstacle to social progress, to enforce it upon the individual by price is an insult to humanity. It is to suppose men suddenly deprived of those higher self-regarding and social instincts, from the free play of which all such morality has sprung, and to deprive them of that sense of responsibility for their own conduct, which is at once the safeguard of life in common, and the earnest of its future development."

But even this inner kernel of law, as it now exists, has been so fatally vitiated by admixtures introduced by the desire to dominate that it is more often opposed to than in accordance with the social sentiments it professes to represent. Take one instance in which the advance of knowledge has come to the aid of struggling social feeling and enlarged our moral sense. I mean the case of so-called criminals. We are now perfectly aware that individuals who commit an outrage upon their fellows are, in the majority of cases, the victims of a defective organisation, or of social arrangements which are a disgrace to our humanity. Yet some of them we brutally murder in cold blood because, in a moment of homicidal mania, they have destroyed human life; others, to whom we have troubled ourselves to give no opportunities of mental or physical development, and who have consequently felt the force of no social obligations, we consign to the tender mercies of a system described by Michael Davitt – after his personal experience of it – as follows,†

> Penal servitude has become so elaborated that it is now a huge punishing machine, destitute through centralised control and responsibility, of discrimination, feeling, or sensitiveness, and its non-success as a deterrent from crime, its complete failure in reformative effect upon criminal character, are owing to its essential tendency to deal with erring human beings – who are still men despite their crimes – in a manner which mechanically reduces them to a uniform level of disciplined brutes.

And all this we acquiesce in, stifling our natural sensations of horror and pity, because it is the work of the law. We confound the fact that the individual who is ignorant enough to run counter to any natural law, whether it be an observed series of sequences in an inanimate nature, or in the social relationships of men must necessarily suffer for his want of understanding; with a sort of crude instinct of retaliation for the infliction of personal inconvenience which still unhappily survives amongst us, and is exactly that which leads a cat to scratch the person who treads upon her tail. Thus we talk with approval of society avenging itself upon the criminal, or rewarding him according to his misdeeds, when the one just attitude of his brother-men towards him, would be that sense of sorrowing sympathy which would lead them to feel themselves in part responsible for the injury done to himself and others, and for its reparation.

---

† *Contemporary Review*, August 1883.

This instance is enough to show what I mean by the vitiation of that small portion of existing law which represents the social sentiments. In truth it has fallen into the hands of the dominators of mankind. It has been formulated by priests, and administered by fighting-men with all the narrowness and cruelty of their crafts until it has practically ceased to represent the moral sense of the people, and become the possession of the privileged classes, who claim the exclusive right of expounding it and carrying it into effect. Moreover they have taken advantage of the respect it commanded to overlay it with a vast mass of regulations in their own interests, for which they have claimed equal reverence, and which exist purely (1st.) to support, define, and defend the monopoly of property (2nd.), to regulate the machinery which upholds it, i.e., Government.

This then is the position of Anarchism at the present moment. It finds itself confronted by the spirit of domination in the concrete form of Property, guarded by law, upheld by the organised force of Government, and backed by the yet undestroyed desire to dominate in certain individuals, ignorance of the issues involved in others, (the majority), and the cowardice, folly, idleness, and selfishness, of mankind in general. In this position what are the practical measures to be taken? What are we Anarchists to do?

To answer this question fully would be to out-step the limits of the present article, for it would be necessary to trace out the relation of the conviction I have been describing to the economic and social tendencies at present existing in society. Now I can only summarise as briefly as possible – necessarily omitting many important considerations.

As a preliminary, we endeavour to discard the principle of domination from our own lives. In the next place, we associate ourselves with others in working for that social revolution, which for us means the destruction of all monopoly and all government, and the direct seizure by the workers of the means of production. It is our aim to give conscious expression to the voiceless cry of the oppressed, believing that as the knowledge of the real causes of their distress slowly dawns upon the victims of despair, with fuller consciousness will come the energy of hope. It is only the incomprehensible which is paralysing. As to the means to be employed – besides the free association of those who share one hope and one belief – they rest with each man's conscience and his opportunities. The employment of force to coerce others is unjustifiable: but as a means of escaping from coercion, if it is available when other means have failed, it is not only excusable, it is a moral obligation. Each man owes it to himself and to society to be free.

Society can relieve itself of monopoly by force; but social re-formation is the work of silent growth, not of conscious, sudden effort, and it may fairly be predicted, that the old will not be thrown off until the new is sufficiently developed to take its place. Already, for the careful and unbiased observer of present tendencies, it is possible to form some conception of the free community of the future. Federated, self-organised, and self-directed trade and distributing societies, voluntary associations of workers, utilising a common capital, and sharing amongst themselves and with one another the produce of their labour, are no startling innovations. But delivered from the yoke of property, which exacts interest, creates monopoly value and competition in consumption, and makes its possessor arbiter of the destiny of his fellows, such associations will obviously exist in a new atmosphere. When each person directs his own life, then, and then only, he throws his whole soul into the work he has chosen, and makes it the expression of his intensest purpose and desire, then, and then only, labour becomes pleasure, and its produce a work of art.

With the cessation of the luxury and misery, which are the exciting causes of crime and vice, and the substitution of a free scope for human energy, it will become possible to treat the decreasing number of criminals, as science and humanity dictate, i.e., as patients suffering from mental or physical aberration, needing the voluntary attention of skilful physicians and nurses. As for the expression of the collective life of the community, and the raising of such members of it as have lagged behind the social standard of conduct, it is enough to note the marvellous growth of public opinion since the emancipation of speech and the press, to become aware that social expressions of opinion and social codes of morality, unsupported by law or Government, are able to exercise a pressure so strong as to be overwhelming, and to take action with a rapidity unrivalled by any police officer. Indeed, they constitute a serious danger to individual freedom, which, as it is a natural result of life in common, can only be met by a higher moral culture.

It follows from what has been said that Anarchism is not a system, but a theory of human development; not a Utopian dream of the future, but a faith for the present; not a nostrum for the cure of all human ills, by the alteration of the material conditions of society, but a protest against certain definite evils, pointed out by reason and experience, as intrenched behind the prejudices of our moral blindness. This protest, this theory, this faith, it carries into every department of life as it is, confident that men will one day see the beauty of life as it might be.

[*The Practical Socialist*, Volume 1, Number 1, January 1886]

What Socialism Is

INTRODUCTION

The last three centuries of English history have been characterised by a political, agricultural and industrial revolution.

At the Reformation, the increasingly important trading class in the cities formed the main strength of the Crown as against the Church and the Baronage. The Civil Wars and the Revolution of 1688-9 placed direct political influence within the reach of this growing middle class; and, from the early part of this century, its wealth has made it the supreme power in the State, through the medium of representative government. Meanwhile, the destruction of the feudal system, consummated by the decimation of the English Baronage in the Wars of the Roses, had tended to place a large portion of the land of the country at the immediate disposal of the King; and the Reformation added the bulk of the territorial possessions of the Church to the estates with which the Tudors were enabled to reward their favorites and supporters. In accordance with the new ideas of property introduced into Northern Europe during that period by the revived influence of Roman law, these estates were granted in private ownership, subject only to the dues to the Crown, abolished in 1645, and replaced in 1660 by a royal revenue raised by general taxation. In these arrangements the claims of the peasantry settled upon the soil from time immemorial were completely ignored. In consequence, these peasants were driven from the land to become hired laborers, vagabonds and paupers. The destruction of the legal rights of the majority of Englishmen in their native soil was completed by the enclosure of common lands, and the removal of small yeomen-farmers to clear the way for large estates farmed by tenants, which took place during the eighteenth and at the beginning of the present century. Thus the English peasantry were transformed into proletarian wage-workers: an instrument ready to the hand of capitalist production.

The discoveries of North and South America and of the passage to India round the Cape of Good Hope, and the era of colonisation which followed opened out new fields for English enterprise. The invention of the steam-engine and of machinery in the eighteenth century completely changed our industrial as well as our agricultural system. The small industries, in which the producer utilised his own capital, were superseded by production on a large scale, with its infinitesimal division of labour, its divorce of capital and the workman, its complete separation of the toil of head and hand, and its competition of capital for profit and of labour for the right to employment. The wars of Napoleon I, checking industry on the Continent, whilst, by raising the price of provisions, they increased agricultural profits at home, enabled England to retain the advantage in commercial development which her inventions had procured her; and, when peace was declared, she was in a position so to utilise the new machinery and facilities of transport and communication as to make herself mistress of the markets of the world. Free trade in corn has enabled her, until lately, to maintain this position; but signs are not wanting that her pre-eminence – and with it high rates of profit for capital, and average sufficiency of employment for wage-labour – is upon the wane.

From this political and economic revolution have sprung alike the enormous increase in our national wealth, and the unsatisfactory nature of its social distribution.

The foundation upon which our modern economic system rests is the monopoly of land and capital (the means of production) by individuals. This monopoly, i.e., *ownership* as distinct from *usufruct*, originated in the ages of violence and open robbery, and is now protected by the legal and political system gradually fabricated for their own security by the monopolist class. The possessors of property in the means of production have thus been enabled to take advantage of the necessities of the propertyless, and to induce them to work on condition of receiving such a share of the produce of their labour as suffices to keep them alive. The man who has nothing but his labour-force, sells that to the owner of land or machinery or raw material, at a price which is always tending to be forced to a lower level by the competition of increasing population. It is true that, on the other hand, this price may be, and sometimes is, raised by the insistence of the workers upon an increased standard of subsistence; but as machinery tends to oust personal skill in labour the mass of unskilled workmen forced to undersell one another for starvation wages continually augments. The existence of this surplus labour in the market is a necessity of capitalist production, since it is only in consequence of competition amongst labourers for work that the capitalist is able to force his workmen to leave him the lion's share of the produce. The difference between the value produced by the workers and the wages they receive is appropriated by the landlord and capitalist class; and each individual landlord or capitalist keeps as much for his personal share as the competition of other owners of land and employers of labour will admit. This competition appears to return a certain amount of surplus value (difference between the produce of labour and its remuneration, absorbed by the non-producing classes as profits, interest, rent, &c.) to the workers as consumers; but increased cheapness of living in one direction, e.g., bread and groceries, tends to be counterbalanced by increased dearness in others, e.g., rent and meat, so that, for the majority of the workers, real wages remain practically at the level of subsistence. Labour combinations, such as Trades Unions and the like, and the higher standard of comfort, upon which so much stress has recently been laid, have only operated by enabling a certain proportion of the more skilful and prudent workers to exact a fluctuating and uncertain advance of wages in particular trades, where personal ability has not yet been superseded by machinery. But the rapid increase of mechanical agency, the alarming development of commercial gambling in its various forms of speculation, manipulation of the money-market, political wire-pulling, over-production, &c., and the recurring periods of alternate inflation and depression which are the necessary result of production for profit, not for use, combine to render the worker's position every day more insecure. In all such cases, he is the helpless and irresponsible victim of the action of others; he has been forced to sell himself for a mess of pottage, and is consequently deprived of the guidance of his own life and the direction of his own labour. For the so-called freedom of contract between wage-payer and wage-receiver is the bargain of Jacob and Esau, in which one party possesses those necessaries of existence that the other must obtain or starve.

But this evolution of economic conditions, fatal to national prosperity, and degrading alike to the idle and to the working population, has brought with it tendencies which are an earnest of remedy. The Great Industry, massing the workers in large cities, and rendering all the branches of production mutually interdependent, has socialised labour and paved the way for co-operation.

The conscious growth of social feeling thus stimulated, and the inevitable development of the representative system towards Democracy, have resulted in State interference on behalf of the exploited class. Education and political power have been the means of suggesting to the oppressed the possibility of changing their social condition by legal methods, and in this direction such English Socialism as exists has hitherto mainly moved.

In other parts of the civilised world the economic problem has been longer and more scientifically discussed, and Socialist opinion has taken shape in two distinct schools, Collectivist and Anarchist. English Socialism is not yet Anarchist or Collectivist, nor yet definite enough in point of policy to be classified. There is a mass of Socialistic feeling not yet conscious of itself as Socialism. But when the unconscious Socialists of England discover their position, they also will probably fall into two parties: a Collectivist party supporting a strong central administration, and a counterbalancing Anarchist party defending individual initiative against that administration. In some such fashion progress and stability will probably be secured under Socialism by the conflict of the ineradicable Tory and Whig instincts in human nature. In view of this probability, the theories and ideals of both parties, as at present formulated, are set forth below; though it must be carefully borne in mind that the majority of English Socialists are not committed to either, but only tend more or less unconsciously in one or other direction.

COLLECTIVISM
Summarised from Bebel's *Woman in the Past, Present and Future*

The monopoly of the means of production being proved by an examination of the history of past and present economic and social development to be the underlying cause of the existing confusion in production and inequality in distribution, Collectivists propose to transfer the control of land and capital to the State; or rather to the community organised administratively; for the State as we know it – an organisation for the maintenance of monopoly – will abolish itself by the act of "expropriating the expropriators". "The government of persons will be replaced by the administration of things."

The machinery of the Collectivist State will consist of executive committees in each local commune or district, representing each branch of industry, elected by universal suffrage for brief periods of office, and paid at the rate of ordinary workmen; and of a central executive committee, consisting of delegates chosen in like manner, or else directly appointed by the local communal councils. These to be supplemented, where necessary, by intermediate provincial committees.

The business of this executive agency will be to calculate the resources of the community and its needs, and, by comparison of the statistics collected, to regulate production according to consumption. Just as such statistics furnish material for the Budget and for the trading enterprises of large firms to-day, they will furnish the standard for social labour in the society of the future. They will determine the daily social labour required from each; and as the amount of this at any given period will depend upon the relation between the development of the needs of society and the advance in the arts of production, and as it will be for the interest of each and all to shorten as much as possible the hours of necessary toil, invention and ingenuity will be thereby as much stimulated as now they are discouraged by the lack of interest of the workers in the introduction of labour-saving appliances and more powerful motors.

Production will be carried on only for the purpose of consumption and not for profit, therefore there will be no buying and selling of commodities. The social value of articles will be measured by the average length of the working time required to produce them under average conditions. The calculated average value of ten minutes of social work in one trade will be exchangeable for ten minutes of social work in another. The labour of each worker will be rewarded according to this estimated average standard, by labour notes or certificates of time; and each may work as long as he finds necessary to supply his individual needs, after which he will be free to employ his time and earnings as he likes. As regards the real equality of this system of remuneration, each is free to choose the productive occupation he prefers; and in conditions which afford to all equal physical and mental advantages, the differences of capacity, where choice of function is allowed, are very slight. In cases, however, in which the supply of labour does not equal the demand, the executive must interfere and re-arrange matters, e.g., in the relative numbers of labourers required in town and country at different seasons of the year. But when regard for human welfare has replaced regard for profit, it will be the interest of all to render every kind of labour both pleasant and safe; and mining, sea-faring, factory-work, &c, will be carried on under scientific, sanitary, and artistic conditions now undreamt of; for their introduction would not repay the individual capitalist. Labour will be directed by foremen elected by the workers, and paid at the same rate; and, as society improves, this office will probably be filled by all in turn.

The exchange of articles of consumption will be effected by communal and district depots under the control of the executive; and thus useless middlemen will be set free for productive labour. This change will also simplify the transport service by preventing the unnecessary passing hither and thither of goods of doubtful utility, and thus the executive will be able to extend the means of transit in such a manner as to facilitate the decentralisation of the population.

The collective possession of land will allow of agriculture being treated as a physical problem on a wider basis than has been possible under the regime of private proprietorship. The highest fertility of the soil does not depend so much on the skill or care expended upon small portions of land as upon topographic conditions only capable of national and international treatment: e.g., elevation, forests, water supply. We are unable to estimate the increase in productiveness obtainable by wholesale improvements in irrigation, drainage, levelling, tree-felling and planting, the alteration of the chemical constituents of soil by the scientific use of sewage and other manures, and so forth, or the freedom from toil such improvements will bring in their train.

Finally, the organisation of society must provide for the needs of the old and sick, and the nurture and education of children from the moment they are weaned until they are of age, education for boys and girls alike being compulsory, physical, intellectual and technical.

As to the immediate methods by which the new social and economic condition is to be introduced, Collectivists are divided into Revolutionists, who disdain all political action, and wait till evolution brings the moment for radical change; and Opportunists, who by political action aim at using the organised force of the State as it is, to transform it into the State as it ought to be.

ANARCHISM
Drawn up by C.M. Wilson, on behalf of the London Anarchists

Anarchism is a theory of human development which lays no less stress than Collectivism upon the economic or materialistic aspect of social relations; but, whilst granting that the immediate cause of existing evils is economic, Anarchists believe that the solution of the social problem can only be wrought out from the equal consideration of the whole of the experience at our command, individual as well as social, internal as well as external. Life in common has developed social instinct in two conflicting directions, and the history of our experience in thought and action is the record of this strife within each individual, and its reflection within each society. One tendency is towards domination; in other words, towards the assertion of the lesser, sensuous self as against the similar self in others, without seeing that, by this attitude, true individuality impoverishes, empties and reduces itself to nonentity. The other tendency is towards equal brotherhood, or to the self-affirmation of fulfilment of the greater and only true and human self, which includes all nature, and thus dissolves the illusion of mere atomic individualism.

Anarchism is the conscious recognition that the first of these tendencies is, and has always been, fatal to real social union, whether the coercion it implies be justified on the plea of superior strength or superior wisdom, of divine right or necessity, of utility or expedience; whether it takes the form of force or fraud, of exacted conformity to an arbitrary legal system or an arbitrary ethical standard, of open robbery or legal appropriation of the universal birthright of land and the fruits of social labour. To compromise with this tendency is to prefer the narrower to the wider expediency, and to delay the possibility of that moral development which alone can make the individual at one in feeling with his fellow, and organic society, as we are beginning to conceive of it, a realisable ideal.

The leading manifestations of this obstructive tendency at the present moment are Property, or the domination over things, the denial of the claim of others to their use; and Authority, the government of man by man, embodied in majority rule; that theory of representation which, whilst admitting the claim of the individual to self-guidance, renders him the slave of the simulacrum that now stands for society.

Therefore, the first aim of Anarchism is to assert and make good the dignity of the individual human being, by his deliverance from every description of arbitrary restraint – economic, political and social; and, by so doing, to make apparent in their true force the real social bonds which already knit men together, and, unrecognised, are the actual basis of such common life as we possess. The means of doing this rest with each man's conscience and his opportunities. Until it is done any definite proposals for the reorganisation of society are absurd. It is only possible to draw out a very general theory as to the probable course of social reconstruction from the observation of growing tendencies.

Anarchists believe the existing organisation of the State only necessary in the interest of monopoly, and they aim at the simultaneous overthrow of both monopoly and State. They hold the centralised "administration of productive processes" a mere reflection of the present middle-class government by representation upon the vague conception of the future.

They look rather for voluntary productive and distributive associations utilising a common capital, loosely federated trade and district communities practising eventually complete free communism in production and consumption. They believe that in an industrial community in which wealth is necessarily a social not an individual product, the only claims which any individual can fairly put forward to a share in such wealth are: firstly, that he needs it: secondly, that he has contributed towards it to the best of his ability: thirdly (as regards any special article), that he has thrown so much of his own personality into its creation that he can best utilise it. When this conception of the relation between wealth and the individual has been allowed to supersede the idea now upheld by force, that the inherent advantage of possessing wealth is to prevent others from using it, each worker will be entirely free to do as nature prompts, i.e., throw his whole soul into the labour he has chosen, and make it the spontaneous expression of his intensest purpose and desire. Under such conditions only labour becomes pleasure and its produce a work of art. But all coercive organisation working with machine-like regularity is fatal to the realisation of this idea. It has never proved possible to perfectly free human beings to co-operate spontaneously with the precision of machines. Spontaneity, or artificial order and symmetry must be sacrificed. And as spontaneity is life, and the order and symmetry of any given epoch only the forms in which life temporarily clothes itself, Anarchists have no fears that in discarding the Collectivist dream of the scientific regulation of industry, and inventing no formulas for social conditions as yet unrealised, they are neglecting the essential for the visionary.

The like reasoning is applicable to the moral aspect of social relations. Crime as we know it is a symptom of the strain upon human fellowship involved in the false and artificial social arrangements which are enforced by authority, and its main cause and sanction will disappear with the destruction of monopoly and the State. Crime resulting from defective mental and physical development can surely be dealt with both more scientifically and more humanely, by fraternal medical treatment and improved education, than by brute force, however elaborated and disguised.

As for the expression of the common life of the community, and the practical persuasion and assistance desirable to raise those who have lagged behind the average of moral development, it is enough to note the marvellous growth of public opinion since the emancipation of platform and press to become aware that no artificial machinery is needful to enforce social verdicts and social codes of conduct without the aid of written laws administered by organised violence. Indeed, when arbitrary restraints are removed, this form of the rule of universal mediocrity is, and has always been, a serious danger to individual freedom; but as it is a natural, not an artificial result of life in common, it can only be counteracted by broader moral culture.

Anarchism is not a Utopia, but a faith based upon the scientific observation of social phenomena. In it the individualist revolt against authority, handed down to us through Radicalism and the philosophy of Herbert Spencer, and the Socialist revolt against private ownership of the means of production, which is the foundation of Collectivism, find their common issue. It is a moral and intellectual protest against the unreality of a society which, as Emerson says, "is everywhere in conspiracy against the manhood of every one of its members". Its one purpose is by direct personal action to bring about a revolution in every department of human existence, social, political and economic. Every man owes it to himself and to his fellows to be free.

[*What Socialism Is*, Fabian Society, Tract Number 4, June 1886]

The Principles and Aims of Anarchists

Charlotte M. Wilson

The key-note of the Anarchist contention is, that the vitiation of social life is produced by the domination of man by man. The spirit of domination is the disintegrating element, which, constantly tending to break up society, is the fundamental cause of confusion and disorder.

This impulse in men to dominate their fellows, i.e., impose their will upon them and assert their own superiority, would seem to be an ignorant misdirection of the healthy impulse to assert human dignity, the unity of man, as distinct but not separate from the unity of nature, and the dignity and spontaneity of the individual human being as distinct but not separate from associated humanity. The misdirection of this impulse has been encouraged by the absence of knowledge as to the nature and method of natural processes, which has resulted in superstitious awe of all uncomprehended manifestations of force in external nature and in man. This awe has been utilised by the stronger and more cunning of the human race to sanction their domination.

As knowledge has penetrated the governed masses, their submission to the oppression of the dominators, whether priests, lawyers, or warriors, has decreased; and the people have revolted against the form of authority then felt most intolerable. This spirit of revolt in the individual and in the masses, is the natural and necessary fruit of the spirit of domination; the vindication of human dignity, and the saviour of social life.

Anarchism is recognition and acknowledgement of this truth, that social peace and the possibility of full social developments depend on the accordance of the equal social claim of each sane adult to the responsibility of guiding his own thoughts, speech and action by the law of his own conscience, and not by the will of any other individual or collection of individuals.

Considering the spirit of domination as the great cause of human misery, and the present disorganisation of social life, Anarchists declare war against its present principal forms of expression – property, and law manufactured and administered by majority rule.

Property is the monopoly of social wealth; the claim to an individual right not only to use such wealth, but to prevent others from using it.

Wealth being the product of the collective labour of society past and present, of associated mankind, can only belong to society. When it is monopolised by the force or cunning of individuals, other individuals who have been prevented by larger and more generous social feeling, want of strength, of ability or opportunity, from monopolising also, must necessarily become subordinate to the monopolists; since they must work to obtain wherewithal to exist, and cannot work without the monopolised instruments of production. Hence the monopoly of social wealth is the main agent of domination.

Its justification on the ground of its social necessity as an inducement to labour, unless forced labour be substituted, is contradicted by the experience of the possibility of voluntary labour for a common object, whether sustenance or social improvements in the common labour of all primitive peoples, of such historical associations as the guilds of the Middle Ages, of the innumerable spontaneous societies and associations for every variety of social effort of the present day. It is also contradicted by scientific observations as to the pleasure experienced by all healthy animals in the exercise of function, and the obvious preference of healthy and free human beings for such occupations as produce a tangible result, satisfy the whole nature morally and physically, and win the approbation of their fellows. Work which is the result of free choice is best done. But the desire to obtain the largest possible share of wealth by labour, injures workmanship and leads to the choice of the most profitable rather than the fittest sort of work.

The monopoly of wealth would have no chance against the sense of social justice and the needs of mankind, unless sanctioned and protected by law.

The kernel of law, which commends it to the respect of the moral sense of men, is the crystallised social custom – result of common experience, social feeling spontaneously called forth by life in common – which our written law contains. But this reasonable respect has been twice converted into superstitious awe by the dominators of men, who have pretended for law the origin of a direct divine revelation, and who have used the reverence thus inspired to cover the whole of the enactments they have made for their own advantage, and the maintenance of their supremacy.

The manufacture and administration of law by the delegates of a majority, changes nothing of its oppressive character; its only purpose remains to impose the will of certain individuals upon the rest, and to maintain certain privileges and distinctions. With the resignation of claim and monopoly of every sort, its occupation is gone.

Apart from this, law is essentially the attempt on the part of certain persons to draw a hard and fast line for the conduct of others; and as the circumstances, motives and personal inspiration of no two individuals is the same, it is a perennial source of injustice and wrong. The pressure and the inspiration which is the natural and inevitable action of the surrounding social atmosphere upon the social sensibilities of the individual, are in all normal cases more than sufficient to secure the possibility of agreement and corporate action. With the removal of arbitrary bonds and hard and fast restraints their strength is more fully recognised, and the aroused sense of responsibility which follows the absence of coercion, tends to make opposition to social claims a matter of conscience rather than of caprice. In abnormal cases, the want of social feeling can be most humanely and more effectually met by an active display of brotherly care and attention; the spirit of resistance to all aggression in the name of human dignity, not of personal self-assertion, and the generous attempt to relieve the physical deformity or disease, or the moral blindness which has led to the aggression.

Anarchism is a protest against the government of man by man in every shape and form as the disturber of social life, an assertion that the free play of the social nature of free and equal human beings is the only solid basis of society.

This is an abstract of paper read before the London Dialectical Society on the 2nd of June [1886].

[*The Present Day*, Number 38 (Old Series), Number 2 (New Series), July 1886]

Freedom

Through the long ages of grinding slavery behind us, Freedom, that unknown goal of human pilgrimage, has hovered, a veiled splendour, upon the horizon of men's hopes. Veiled in the trembling ignorance of mankind, their misty unreasoning terror of all that revealed itself as power, whether it were an apparently incomprehensible and uncontrollable natural force, or the ascendancy of superior strength, ability or cunning in human society. The inward attitude of slavish adoration towards what imposes itself from without as a fact beyond our understanding, that is the veil which hides Freedom from the eyes of men. Sometimes it takes the form of the blind fear of a savage of his "medicine" or his fetish, sometimes of the equally blind reverence of an English workman for the law of his masters, and the semblance of consent to his own economic slavery wormed out of him by the farce of representation. But whatever the form the reality is the same, ignorance, superstitious terror, cowardly submission.

What is human progress but the advance of the swelling tide of revolt against this tyranny of the nightmare of ignorant dread, which has held men the slaves of external nature, of one another, and of themselves? Science and the arts, knowledge and all its varied shapes of practical application by ingenuity and skill, the binding and enlightening force of affection and social feeling, the protest of individuals and of peoples by word and deed against religious, economic, political and social oppression, these, one and all, are weapons in the hands of the Rebels against the Powers of Darkness sheltered behind their shield of authority, divine and human. But they are weapons not all equally effective at all times. Each has its period of special utility.

We are living at the close of an era during which the marvellous increase of knowledge left social feeling behind, and enabled the few who monopolised the newly acquired power over nature to create an artificial civilisation, based upon their exclusive claim to retain private, personal possession of the increased wealth produced.

Property – not the claim to use, but to a right to prevent others from using – enables individuals who have appropriated the means of production, to hold in subjection all those who possess nothing but their vital energy, and who must work that they may live. No work is possible without land, materials, and tools or machinery; thus the masters of these things are the masters also of the destitute workers, and can live in idleness upon their labour, paying them in wages only enough of the produce to keep them alive, only employing so many of them as they find profitable and leaving the rest to their fate.

Such a wrong once realised is not to be borne. Knowledge cannot long be monopolised, and social feeling is innate in human nature, and both are fomenting within our hide-bound Society as the yeast in the dough. Our age is on the eve of a revolt against property, in the name of the common claim of all to a common share in the results of the common labour of all.

Therefore, we are Socialists, disbelievers in Property, advocates of the equal claims of each man and woman to work for the community as seems good to him or her – calling no man master, and of the equal claim of each to satisfy as seems good to him, his natural needs from the stock of social wealth he has laboured to produce. We look for this socialisation of wealth, not to restraints imposed by authority upon property, but to the removal, by the direct personal action of the people themselves, of the restraints which secure property against the claims of popular justice. For authority and property both are manifestations of the egoistical spirit of domination, and we do not look to Satan to cast out Satan.

We have no faith in legal methods of reform. Fixed and arbitrary written law is, and has always been, the instrument employed by anti-social individuals to secure their authority, whether delegated or usurped, when the maintenance of that authority by open violence has become dangerous. Social feeling, and the social habits formed and corrected by common experience, are the actual cement of associated life. It is the specious embodiment of a portion of this social custom in law, which has made law tolerable, and even sacred in the eyes of the people it exists to enslave. But in proportion as the oppression of law is removed, the true binding force of the influence of social feeling upon individual responsibility becomes apparent and is increased. We look for the destruction of monopoly, not by the imposition of fresh artificial restraints, but by the abolition of all arbitrary restraints whatever. Without law, property would be impossible, and labour and enjoyment free.

Therefore, we are Anarchists, disbelievers in the government of man by man in any shape and under any pretext. The human freedom to which our eyes are raised is no negative abstraction of licence for individual egoism, whether it be massed collectively as majority rule or isolated as personal tyranny. We dream of the positive freedom which is essentially one with social feeling; of free scope for the social impulses, now distorted and compressed by Property, and its guardian the Law; of free scope for that individual sense of responsibility, of respect for self and for others, which is vitiated by every form of collective interference, from the enforcing of contracts to the hanging of criminals; of free scope for the spontaneity and individuality of each human being, such as is impossible when one hard and fast line is fitted to all conduct. Science is teaching mankind that such crime as is not the manufacture of our vile economic and legal system, can only be rationally as well as humanely treated by fraternal medical care, for it results from deformity or disease, and a hard and fast rule of conduct enforced by condign punishment is neither guide nor remedy, nothing but a perennial source of injustice amongst men.

We believe each sane adult human being to possess an equal and indefeasible claim to direct his life from within by the light of his own consciousness, to the sole responsibility of guiding his own action as well as forming his own opinions. Further, we believe that the acknowledgement of this claim is a necessary preliminary to rational voluntary agreement, the only permanent basis of harmonious life in common. Therefore, we reject every method of enforcing assent, as in itself a hindrance to effectual co-operation, and further, a direct incentive to anti-social feeling. We deprecate as a wrong to human nature, individually, and therefore collectively, all use of force for the purpose of coercing others; but we assert the social duty of each to defend, by force if need be, his dignity as a free human being, and the like dignity in others, from every form of insult and oppression.

We claim for each and all the personal right and social obligation to be free. We hold the complete social recognition and acknowledgement of such a claim to be the goal of human progress in the future, as its growth has been the gauge of development of Society in the past, of the advance of man from the blind social impulse of the gregarious animal to the conscious social feeling of the free human being.

Such, in rough outline, is the general aspect of the Anarchist Socialism our paper is intended to set forth, and by the touchstone of this belief we purpose to try the current ideas and modes of action of existing Society.

[*Freedom*, Volume 1, Number 1, October 1886]

Work

"In the sweat of thy brow shalt thou eat bread" is an ancient curse, dating from the days of slavery. And truly for the slave work is a weariness to the flesh.

What enjoyment is there in his labour for the modern wage-slave, for instance, as he toils hour after hour and day after day at some exhausting routine work, in which he sees no special utility, and for which he has no special taste; toils wearily on and on, with no prospect but the same dull round, until he breaks down and is sent to the work-house, like some worn-out cart-horse to the knackers? How can work be anything but a hateful burden in such circumstances? How can such workers have any inclination but to exert themselves as little as possible? Any interest but the amount of the miserable pittance they gain by this prostitution of their manhood? No wonder that to the majority of the workmen of to-day wages are the one inducement to work, and the idea of working except for wages seems an absurdity. No wonder that when they can avoid working, they loaf, or that they seek physical or mental relief for their deadened and jaded nerves in spirits or beer or gambling.

The nature of the modern machine industry and factory system is in itself enough to account for the so-called idleness of the working classes; but there are many other causes which all unite to render the very idea of work distasteful to the masses at this moment.

Manual work is looked on as a brand of inferiority to the worker. Whatever his skill, he is regarded as belonging to the lower rank in society. Cap in hand he stands meekly before the brain-worker, the organiser, the mere monopolist of property, awaiting their permission to employ himself and their direction of his efforts. He is their hireling, their thing, a part of their wealth-producing machinery. How can he joy in the toil which degrades him in the eyes of his fellows and is associated with the loss of his personal dignity?

And then he is never secure even in this inferior position, which at least allows him to live. Any week, any day he may be thrown upon the streets to beg from door to door for the permission to work that he may earn a subsistence. This insecurity nips in the bud such growing interest as he may be inclined to feel in his special occupation. He may be interested in finishing some job, in thinking out some improvement, but all the while the knowledge lurks in the background that he has neither part nor lot in the final utility of his work, that to-morrow he may be a homeless wanderer, his connection with his present employment broken off for ever.

So much for the character of the work; let us turn to the physical conditions of the lives of the workers. Insufficient food from earliest childhood; if not insufficient in quantity, insufficient in nourishing elements, unwholesome and adulterated, as are all the wretched provisions sold in the cheap shops of our large towns. Insufficient clothing; shoddy cotton and cloth, and paper soled boots, and not enough even of these. Bad air; dirty, badly ventilated factories and workshops all day, damp or dusty ill-smelling streets to go home by, hot, close rooms to sit and eat and sleep in. Such conditions alone are enough to depress the nervous energy of the strongest and healthiest amongst us, and men and women who have lived for generations in such misery are not strong and healthy. A moment's reflection astonishes us not at the idleness but the industry of the working classes.

But the property monopolists? There is a strong tendency amongst them also to believe that the only end of useful effort is to fill one's own pocket, and a pronounced distaste for work in itself; and yet their lives are not fettered like those of their wage-slaves.

Not in the same way, but still fettered, and by the same hateful social system. The majority of men and women of whatever class have capacity for hand-work. Those whose organisation fits them exclusively for brain work are few and far between. Yet the iron tyranny of custom ordains that for a man or woman of the upper classes brain work alone is "respectable"; they must exercise their muscles only in games. If such a person is caught by his neighbours in the act of digging potatoes, or scrubbing the floor, or making any useful article, he or she apologises with a blush and explains that it is only a hobby, or he has been obliged to do it "just for once" by some accident. As to bringing up his children as shoemakers or cooks, he would as soon educate them for the hulks. And yet not every bourgeois child has a taste for figures, or the organisation of industry, or scientific research, or the higher walks of art.

Again, the weight and pressure of needless clothing, and curtained rooms, and padded seats, and a hot-house atmosphere, and luxurious living, and artificial isolation from the first elementary needs and cares of humanity, are not healthy, are not in the truest sense natural. Such conditions depress nervous energy and discourage exertion, and make the real interests and larger purposes of life dull and meaningless. And such conditions as these have grown up around the rich, punishing them for their unjust monopoly by enervating their nerves and stupefying their brain, shutting them away from the keen, fresh pleasure of living, and turning work and repose alike to weariness.

And if the enervating and isolating "comfort" of the rich and the cramping and depressing misery of the poor, the difficulty for either class of choosing the occupation which best suits them, and the dreary and monotonous character of most modern labour, were causes not sufficient to account for such disinclination to useful and continued exertion of energy as we see around us, we have only to add the social influence of an idle aristocracy. The example of an upper class whose pride is that for many hundred years they have been absolutely useless, cannot but corrupt the whole community. They set before every man an ideal of idleness as the goal to which all his labour should tend; so that for the hand workers and commercial class being a gentleman means that, being rich, one has nothing to do, and to many of them the object of working is to attain such gentility as fate will allow.

For the taskmaster as for the slave there is but little joy in labour, and our social conditions make most men and women one or the other. Little cause have we for surprise that idleness is no uncommon vice amongst all classes and that but too many men are ready to cast their burden of toil upon the shoulders of others.

But now let us contrast this distaste for work, this tendency to shirk it which is the direct outcome of present social conditions, with the mighty volume of active energy, which, in spite of these adverse conditions, actually animates society from day to day.

This display of spontaneous energy in useful work is such a common factor of ordinary life that it passes unnoticed, until something rouses us to reflect that our whole social progress depends on it and that if it ceased for one single day society would come to a stand-still, even though all slavish labour went on as before. I do not dwell here upon the endless voluntary associations for every imaginable object, public or private, from the reform of society or the protection of vested interests to the exercise of the muscles or the amusement of leisure moments. Of course these involve a very large amount of unpaid and avoidable exertion; but the energy summed up in them is but as a drop in the bucket compared with the free, spontaneous effort ceaselessly expended in the common daily work of life; effort which can never be measured, never be paid for, and for which we can find no definite, determining necessity, unless we look for it in the inmost nature of man himself.

One begins to realise this if one tries to imagine the results to any sort of work if the spontaneous human element were entirely excluded. The capitalist machine industry has done its best in this direction, and in proportion as it has succeeded, the produce has grown not only mean and base but useless and hurtful. In proportion as the human worker has become a mere steam-engine with wages for coal, the fruit of his labour has degenerated into shoddy, losing not only the higher utility, the beauty that satisfies the mind, but the most elementary fitness to supply primary needs. Our tin teapots for instance, not only degrade our imagination and deform our sense of proportion by their hideousness, but they melt on the hob, they leak when boiling water is poured into them, and they poison us with the leaden "tea tasters" in the spout; our cheap cottons are not only frightful in their stiffness and mean in their flimsiness, but they neither wash nor wear; and so on.

It is only amongst the weakest and most stunted victims of industrialism that we see what sort of thing human labour is when the spontaneous element is utterly crushed out of it. Even amidst the most degraded and hopeless routine work, spontaneous energy is often only diverted from ingenuity to speed, and concentrated upon producing the greatest quantity possible, regardless of quality. In many a hard-driven workman the impulse to produce is so strong, that if he can do nothing else, he will find satisfaction in putting, e.g., as many poisonous lumps of lead as possible into the spouts of teapots and joy in beating the record, even though the increased pay be infinitesimally small and he knows that he is merely raising the intensity of labour that will eventually be exacted from him by the capitalists. It is this impulse to put one's best self into what one is doing quite as much as the desire to earn, which is so vilely exploited by employers in all piece work.

The same spontaneous impulse manifests itself in the perpetual improvements and inventions made by workmen. These ceaseless minor inventions are one of the great main springs of economic progress. The workers personally gain nothing by their ingenuity but loss or uncertainty of employment, yet they are always improving and inventing.

In every condition of life people are constantly exerting themselves more than they are compelled to by any external necessity; from the artist like Watts, who pours his whole soul into pictures the public will neither buy nor appreciate, to the dustman who carefully fills the corners of his cart and pats down the edges of his load, though the Vestry will never pay him one penny the more for it. In fact we are not all ourselves conscious, when we come to think of it, that we continually do things for the mere pleasure of doing them or of attaining some end that cannot be measured in hard cash; and also that in work which is paid we perpetually exert ourselves far more than we are absolutely obliged to do to earn our money.

In healthy children the impulse to make something is one of their earliest and most vigorous developments. If they cannot do anything else, they will make mud pies. But most children are far the most eager to do something "real", by which they mean socially useful. They eagerly aspire to the dignity of taking active part in the occupations of grown up people; but till the idea is put into their heads, even the children of this commercial age are not so corrupted by heredity as to think of payment. They obey their own spontaneous impulse to exert themselves to some purpose, just for the pleasure of it.

Physiologists explain to us how this comes about. How exertion of brain and nerves and muscles in work is an exercise of functions and faculties which nature has formed to be exercised, so that there is just as much animal pleasure in working when one is well and strong, as in eating when one is hungry. Starvation of the impulse to work is a physical misery, just like starvation of the impulse to eat. We say impulse to work, rather than merely to exert one's self, because useless or purposeless exertion does not satisfy the mind, and the same may be said of work which is not, at least indirectly, social in character.

If this seems somewhat doubtful to any overworked reader, let him remember the misery of prisoners in solitary confinement. When the nervous exhaustion following the excitement of the trial has passed away, the prisoner's strongest desire is to be allowed some occupation; any work however disagreeable, so that he may escape from the maddening irritation of enforced idleness. And if the deprivation is long continued, the strongest man will sink into a semi-idiotic condition of bodily and mental apathy, just as one of our arms will first be cramped and then become feeble and nerveless if it be tied up and not exercised.

Another consideration suggests the existence of a spontaneous impulse amongst men to produce, to create. It is the enormous wealth which the human race has acquired beyond what is necessary for bare subsistence. Think, for example, of the means of communication, from language to railways and steam-boats, and try to realise the volume of creative energy they imply, not in a few individuals, but in the millions whose labours of mind and body have formed them during long ages. If men had contented themselves with merely providing for their bare necessities, none of the arts of life would have grown and developed, and we should still be existing like our ancestors, the cave men. But no, the cave men have left behind them evidences of their human creative genius. We find their stone and bone knives and hatchets, not only sharpened, but shaped and ornamented, and since their day we have gone on shaping and ornamenting, and thinking and creating, until we have accumulated the vast stores of knowledge and of material wealth amidst which we live to-day. Where was the compulsion to do all this, but in our own nature?

There is little room to doubt, when one thinks seriously about the matter, that the expenditure of energy in creation, in productive work, is a natural human impulse, common to all normally developed individuals, and idleness a disease developed and fostered by unhealthy conditions. Therefore the question of supreme importance in social organisation is – not how can men be induced to work, but how can their spontaneous desire to work be allowed the freest scope and guided into the most useful directions.

[*Freedom*, Volume 2, Number 22, July 1888]

Democracy or Anarchism

It is surely a somewhat arbitrary definition of the word Socialism to use it as a term of exclusion for the complete socialisation of all wealth, viz., Communism, and to confine it to the partial socialisation of wealth aimed at by certain Socialists who would limit their endeavours to the socialisation of land and certain of the agents of production. This sort of Socialism is obviously a compromise between the idea of the absolute individual right to monopolise wealth, i.e., to prevent others from using what one calls one's own, whether one is using it or not, and the idea of the common and equal claim of all to the use of the collective wealth of the whole society.

We are living exactly at the moment when the conflict between these two ideas of right and justice in economics is beginning to wax hot and strong and is rapidly becoming general throughout civilised society, and the sort of Socialism referred to is the natural creed of all peaceable folks, who convinced of the injustice and woeful consequences of private property or individualism in economics, are prepared to introduce the new or rather the growing idea of social justice as gradually and smoothly as possible; a sort of boring of the rock that has fallen athwart the stream of human progress. Some people seem to incline to bore it with a gimlet. As the idea of land nationalisation was the thin end of the wedge which opened a way for the idea of the socialisation of capital, so the idea of the socialisation of those means of production which afford a special instrument of exploitation when monopolised, is opening a path for the socialisation of all wealth. And the word Socialism, though it covers all these approximations to common ownership, should also, and of greater right, cover that Communism which is their logical and natural result.

We do not use the word Democracy in the vague and poetic sense in which it is employed, by Walt Whitman and Edward Carpenter, for the whole progress of mankind from political, economic and social bondage towards liberty, equality and fraternity, but according to its exact political meaning – the rule or government of the many. Democracy is the natural and inevitable political form of the period of economic transition in which we are now living – for it too is a compromise – a transition phase of thought between two definite principles of human association.

There are two definite principles, on which human beings can associate for any purpose whatever, the principle of authority and the principle of free consent. Men associate on the understanding that one or some of them have a claim to over-rule the opinions or the actions or both of the others, or they associate on the understanding that they are all equals, meeting on equal terms, each one having as much claim as the rest to think and act on his own initiative, and therefore that common action must be decided upon unanimously. As far as we can judge human association began unconsciously on this latter principle. And after passing through a long phase of development, during which authority first became paramount, unconsciously, and was afterwards consciously adopted as a principle of social order, it would appear that humanity is returning to the association of free consent, but this time consciously and of deliberate intention, to escape the evils of the other system.

What we call the Saxon period in English history was one long struggle of the principle of authority in association against the principle of free consent; of the efforts of the land-grabbers to obtain ascendancy in the folk moots of the village communities and the larger moots of the various federations, and of the biggest practising land-grabber who made himself king, to secure the ascendancy of himself and his companions in arms in all the public business of the community which, it would appear, was being carried on without his interference on the basis of free association and unanimity. We have scarcely any records of the working of the old principle in the purity of its unconscious ascendancy, we see its strength only in the long struggle that was made to retain it, re-appearing again (as in the guilds and the early days of the free cities) every time that anything like economic equality was restored in any section of society. The jury is a vestige of it that has lingered in a curious distorted medium down to our own times. In less civilised communities, in the mir in Russia and the hill communities of India for example, we see it still remaining in its ancient form – in Russia curiously overlaid by one of the foulest examples of the rival principle that history has furnished.

Of the dolorous history of that rival principle of authority we need no examples. We all know how the wretched fate of humanity has led us through the rule of a number of small tyrants, distinguished by strong muscles, to the rule of one big tyrant distinguished by superior cunning, and then again to the rule of a minority distinguished by superior capacities for land-grabbing and wealth-appropriating in general till it has landed us in the rule of the large minority of property holders over the propertyless masses. Each of these forms of over-rule has fought desperately both in the spiritual and the material sense with the form preceding it: first for bare survival and then for supremacy, and each has prolonged its existence far into the over-lordship of its successor. At the present moment the recently victorious plutocracy is engaged in a conflict for dear life with that strange, shapeless monster, called vaguely democracy, which from being the obedient support and catspaw of the rule of the rich, has lately threatened to transform its accustomed gullible stupidity into an unknown aspect of threatening defiance.

Democracy is the political theory that assumes that all members of a community meet as equals on equal terms, but that nevertheless the majority have an absolute right to over-rule the minority. And it is worth while to look closely into the real significance of this curious non sequitur, which starting with the formula of free association ends with the formula of authority.

Where does the majority get its absolute right from? Right is a dubious word that one gets in the way of using without explanation; but I suppose that we mean by it in a general way, a claim put forward by members of a society and allowed by the rest, either because they feel it to be just or because they are afraid or unwilling to contest it – a socially recognised claim in fact. It is often said that men have no rights as against one another individually and collectively but such as they are able to maintain by superior force. And I think that though this barbarous and inhuman theory is perfectly untrue of many social rights, it is the universal explanation of the acceptance of a claim to rule. But can majority rule claim its right on these grounds?

Is it not a plain and obvious truth that supremacy in brute force by no means rests with the majority. History and daily life show us examples thick as blackberries of an energetic and resolute minority utterly defeating the majority in the most desperate trials of actual physical strength, ever since the days when a handful of Greeks defeated the mighty hosts of Persia on the plain of Marathon and Horatius and his two comrades held the Tiber bridge against the army of Lars Porsena. Providence fights on the side of the strongest battalion, but not by any means on those of the largest. And this is even more obviously true when the contest is transferred to the intellectual field.

No; the history of authority has consisted of a series of minority rules, each one of which has existed in virtue of the superior possession of the real strength of vital energy in one form or another. And where is the evidence that the dominating force is about to become or is becoming the portion of the majority? The majority today retains the relation it has always retained to the energetic minority of the population. It represents the dead blight of a blind adherence to habit and custom, of insensibility, dullness and apathy, of lazy inclination to avoid all responsibility, all reform, all enlightenment, in fact all departure from the beaten track, all need for unwonted exertion even in thought. If it is to exercise authority it will exercise it only by the dead weight of inertia, the blind force of unreasoning and irresponsible stupidity – in the sense, in fact, in which it exercises it now and always has exercised it.

No doubt "the public collectively", as Mill says, "is abundantly ready to impose not only its generally narrow views of its own interests, but its abstract opinion and even its tastes upon individuals". And if it has machinery at command for doing this without trouble it will oppress without mercy. Do you think that the majority of American citizens were any more unwilling that the Chicago men or John Brown should be hanged than the majority of Jews that Christ should be crucified? Do you think that a plebiscite of London citizens, or the inhabitants of England would maintain the right of meeting in Trafalgar Square? In the name of human progress and the spontaneous individual initiative on which it depends, we may thank our stars that the majority as yet show no sign of acquiring that right to rule founded on superior force. But if the theory of democracy or the rule of the majority cannot be based on the appeal to force which has been the basis of all other over-ruling, what, then is its basis? Shall we say expediency? It is a first approximation – a blundering attempt to return to the principle of free association, still hampered by the ideas of authority yet current in society. On all occasions for common action, or where a general understanding is desirable, one must have some principle of decision and the recent development of social feeling has rendered an appeal to the old species of authority as morally odious, as it is intellectually contemptible. It is a matter of common experience that men, like sheep and all other gregarious and social animals, have a pretty general tendency to go in masses and act together unless they are prevented by some abnormal division of interests. Each one of us is inclined by our social feeling to like in a general way to do what the rest like. In ninety-nine cases out of a hundred where a number of people are met together to decide upon some common course of conduct, they will all in the end come to some definite decision in favour of one thing; because those who were at one time inclined to dissent, prefer in the end to act with the majority, if the matter is of practical importance; not because they are forced to do so by the majority over-ruling, but because the largest body of opinion has so much weight with them that they choose not to act contrary to it.

We all admit this general fact. It would be quite impossible to take any common action at all if it were not so. But the special theory of democracy is that the general tendency of humanity which becomes so apparent whenever men associate on anything like terms of economic equality, should be made by men into an arbitrary law of human conduct to be enforced not only in the ninety-nine cases where nature enforces it, but by the arbitrary methods of coercion in the hundredth where she doesn't. And for the sake of the hundredth case, for the sake of enforcing this general natural tendency where nature does not enforce it, democrats would have us retain in our political relation that fatal principle of the authority of man over man which has been the cause of confusion and disorder, of wrong and misery in human societies since the dawn of history.

"Men are not social enough to do without it," it has been said. For our part we do not know when they will be social enough to do *with* it. Experience has not yet revealed the man who could be safely trusted with power over his fellows; and majority rule is nothing else in practice than putting into the hands of ambitious individuals the opportunity to crush their fellows by the dead weight of the blind mass of which we have spoken. If the principle of authority in human association survives the destruction of the plutocracy, the next ruling minority will probably be the wits and apostles of reason-worship. But we do not think they will have a long innings, even if they ever take their turn in the field at all. The real strength of democracy, its real terror for the ruling-classes of to-day, its real hold over the minds of the people lies in the fact that after all it is but the somewhat uncouth and misleading mask beneath which the principle of free and equal association is advancing to victory. The so-called advent of democracy means not that authority is transferred from the minority to the majority, but that authority is dying, and the masses and each individual man and woman of them, are preparing to throw off the yoke of property and authority together and assume the attitude of equality – politically as well as economically.

It is a commonplace to say that every man who chooses has thrown off the yoke of authority, even of majority rule in matters of opinion; and generally speaking it is true, in spite of the occasional bursts of atavism in the form of some petty persecution. It is needless to dwell on the growing disrespect for the existing forms of authority in every relation of life. Let us only instance the change of spirit which has come over one sort of association – the smallest possible – that of marriage. Fifty years ago it would have been a scandal to deny the authority of the husband over the wife. Association would be impossible on any other terms than the authority of one of the partners, said the superior wisdom of the nation; and yet now, despite the prayer-book and the lawyers, anyone in the more enlightened society of our time who disputed the perfect equality of the man and woman as regards a right to decide on their common interests and action, would be looked on as a barbarian. It is only one instance of a change of attitude which permeates the whole public opinion of our time.

Briefly, then, let us note what line the political organisation is likely to take in a state of society where the principle of authority in all forms of association – in action as well as in opinion – is no longer recognised as *moral* or *just*. First, it will be decentralised. Except in moments of extraordinary popular excitement, when a whole people may be said spontaneously to act as one man, we cannot have a centralised administration of public affairs by unanimity. That ancient tendency to the local management of affairs which has been mixed up with the principle of free association all through our history and is now declaring itself in the present attitude of Ireland, Scotland and Wales, in the demands for a local government bill, local government for London, etc., will take much wider scope. Each town, village, locality, each trade and craft and art knows its own needs and affairs best, and each such group like each individual man can serve humanity in general best by themselves setting about what they see wants doing in their locality – instead of either sending someone else to do it elsewhere, or waiting for orders or permission from any central authority before beginning to act. Each commune, each association, will settle their own general affairs amongst themselves, every sane, grown-up person in the society having an equal voice in deciding what is to be done. This sort of decision by unanimity does not take so long or require so much patience after all when people know that they must reach such a decision on pain of losing some advantage and that they have no means of coercion to force their individual will or wills on their fellows.

But public business includes not only local affairs but matters of general concern to all the communes of a nation, not to speak of international federation of nations. How shall we manage them?

How are they managed now?

Each commune concerned will, we think, meet and discuss the affair in question and then send one or two of their number to meet like delegates from the other localities concerned. The congress will discuss the particular business in hand and after arriving at some general decision, the delegates who have each represented the ideas of their own locality, will return to their own communes, not with laws in their pockets to be enforced with soldiers and machine guns, or even "moral miracles in blue", but with proposals for some line of common action, as scientists or commercial men return from a congress now. Proposals which are not acceptable to the commune will not be acted on, but further discussed until some common understanding can be arrived at. The delay will be less costly in human effort and human suffering than any system of coercion.

[*Freedom*, Volume 4, Number 39, February 1890]

Anarchism and Homicidal Outrage

The Freedom Group

"The propagandists of anarchist doctrines will be treated with the same severity as the actual perpetrators of outrage." – Telegram from Barcelona, *Times*, Nov. 10 [1893]

Is the above quoted decision of the Spanish Government a measure for the protection of human life, justified by the peculiar doctrines of Anarchism? Or is it merely one of those senseless and cruel persecutions of new ideas distasteful to the class in power, that may be expected in the ancient home of the Inquisition?

This question must have struck many thoughtful men and women in England, who have heard for the first time of Anarchism as existing in their midst through the recent vituperations of the capitalist press, and certain Conservative members of the House of Commons. And we, the publishing group of the oldest and most widely circulated Communist Anarchist paper in England, wish to meet this question fairly and frankly, and in reply to plainly state our own convictions on the subject.

Human beings have sometimes held beliefs of which murder was the logical and necessary outcome, as, for instance, the Thugs in India, who looked upon the murder of travellers as a religious obligation: is Anarchism such a belief? If it is, then the Spanish people are certainly justified in clearing their country of Anarchists; even though the perpetration of the Barcelona outrage be never directly traced to them; and the English people will be justified in regarding their Anarchist countrymen as enemies, dangerous in proportion as they are energetic and sincere.

We propose to enquire, firstly, if homicidal outrage is the logical outcome of Anarchist principles; secondly, if such outrage is a necessary method in the practical attempt to introduce Anarchism as a principle of conduct, a transforming agency, into existing society; thirdly, we propose to give our view of homicidal outrage as an actual social phenomenon, the existence of which, whatever be its cause, cannot be disputed.

I. – Is homicidal outrage the logical outcome of Anarchist* convictions?
The Communist Anarchist looks upon human societies as, essentially,
natural groups of individuals, who have grown into association for the
sake of mutually aiding one another in self-protection and self-
development. Artificially formed Empires, constructed and held together
by force, he regards as miserable shams. The societies he recognises are
those naturally bound together by real sympathies and common ideas and
aims. And in his eyes, the true purpose of every such natural society,
whether it be a nation or a federation of nations, a tribe or a village
community, is to give to every member of it the largest possible
opportunities in life. The object of associating is to increase the
opportunities of the individual. One isolated human being is helpless, a
hopeless slave to external nature; whereas the limits of what is possible to
human beings in free and rational association are as yet unimagined.

Now the Anarchist holds a natural human society good in proportion as
it answers what he believes to be its true purpose, and bad in proportion
as it departs from that purpose, and instead of enlarging the lives of the
individuals composing it crushes and narrows them.

For instance, when in England a comparatively few men claim a right to
exclusive possession of the soil, and thereby prevent others from enjoying
or using it except upon hard and stinting terms, the Anarchist says that
English Society, in so far as it recognises such an arrangement, is bad and
fails of its purpose; because such an arrangement instead of enlarging the
opportunities for a full human life for everybody, cruelly curtails them for
all agricultural workers and many others, and moreover is forced on the
sufferers against their will, and not arrived at, as all social arrangements
ought to be, by mutual agreement.

Such being his view of human societies in general, the Anarchist, of
course, endeavours to find out, and make clear to himself and others, the
main causes why our own existing society is here and now failing so
dismally, in many directions, to fulfil its true function. And he has arrived
at the conclusion that these causes of failure are mainly two. First, the
unhappy recognition of the authority of man over man as a morally right
principle, a thing to be accepted and submitted to, instead of being resisted
as essentially evil and wrong. And second, the equally unhappy

---

* When using the term Anarchism in this article we throughout mean Communist or
Socialistic Anarchism, and under the term "homicidal outrage", we are, of course, not
dealing with violence used in direct and immediate self-defence.

recognition of the right of property, i.e., the right of individuals, who have complied with certain legal formalities, to monopolise material things, whether they are using them or need to use them or not, and whether they have produced them or not. To the Anarchist, the state of the public conscience which permits these two principles of authority and property to hold sway in our social life seems to lie at the root of our miserably desocialised condition; and therefore he is at war with all institutions and all habits which are based on these principles or tend to keep them up. He is not the enemy of society, never of society, only of anti-social abuses.

He is not the enemy of any man or set of men, but of every system and way of acting which presses cruelly upon any human being, and takes away from him any of the chances nature may have allowed him of opportunities equal to those of his fellow men.

Such, in general terms, is the mental attitude of the Anarchist towards Society, and beneath this attitude, at the root of these theories and beliefs lies something deeper: a sense of passionate reverence for human personality; that new-born sense – perhaps the profoundest experience which the ages have hitherto revealed to man – which is yet destined to transform human relations and the human soul; that sense which is still formless and inexpressible to most of us, even those whom it most strongly stirs, and to which Walt Whitman has given the most adequate, and yet a most inadequate and partial voice:

Each of us inevitable,
Each of us limitless – each of us with his or her right upon the earth,
Each of us allow'd the eternal purports of the earth,
Each of us here as divinely as any is here.

Is this an attitude of heart and mind which must logically lead a man on to commit homicidal outrage? With such feelings, with such convictions must we not rather attach a peculiar sanctity to human life? And, in fact, the genuine Anarchist looks with sheer horror upon every destruction, every mutilation of a human being, physical or moral. He loathes wars, executions and imprisonments, the grinding down of the worker's whole nature in a dreary round of toil, the sexual and economic slavery of women, the oppression of children, the crippling and poisoning of human nature by the preventable cruelty and injustice of man to man in every shape and form. Certainly, this frame of mind and homicidal outrage cannot stand in the relation of cause and effect.

II. – Though Anarchist principles do not in themselves logically lead to the commission of homicidal outrages, do they practically drive the active Anarchist into this course by closing other means of action?
It is true that his convictions close to the conscientious Anarchist one form of social action, just now unfortunately popular, i.e., parliamentary agitation.

He cannot conscientiously take part in any sort of government, or try to relieve the cruel pressure upon human lives by means of governmental reforms, because one of the worst possible evils he could do his fellow men would, in his eyes, be to strengthen their idea that the rule of man over man is a right and beneficial thing. For, of course, every well-meant attempt of the men in power to better things tends to confirm people in the belief that to have men in power is, after all, not a social evil. Whereas the aim of the Anarchist is to convince his fellow men that authority is no essential part of human association, but a disruptive element rather, and one to be eliminated, if we would have social union without unjust and unequal social pressure. The current political means of action and protest, therefore, are barred to the Anarchist, by the new-born conception of social relations which is the key-note of his creed. On this point he differs from all other Socialists and social reformers.

But is homicide the necessary antithesis of parliamentary agitation? Must the man who looks upon political action, as commonly understood, as useless and worse, necessarily endeavour to spread his views or improve society by outrages upon his fellow-men?

The question is obviously absurd. If one particular way is barred, an infinite variety of other ways are open. The great changes in the world's history, the great advances in human development have not been either set a-going or accomplished by the authority of kings and rulers, but by the initiative of this man and that in making fresh adaptations to changing material conditions, and by the natural and voluntary association of those who saw, or even blindly felt the necessity for a new departure. And now, as always, the great social change which the most callous feel to be at our doors, is springing from the masses, the inmost depths of the nation in revolt against unendurable misery, and fired with a new hope of better things. We Anarchists have the whole of this vast sphere for our action: – the natural and voluntary social life of our countrymen. Not a society founded on principles of voluntary association for any useful purpose whatever, but our place is there. Not a natural human relationship, but it is our work to infuse it with a new spirit. Is not this field wide enough for the zeal of the most fiery propagandist? More particularly in England, at this moment, we find as a field for our endeavours the vast force of the organised labour movement; a force which, rightly applied, could here and now bring about the economic side of the Social Revolution. Not the parliament, not the government, but the organised workmen of England – that minority of the producers who are already organised – *could*, if they would, and if they knew how, put an end to capitalist exploitation, landlord monopoly, to the starvation of the poor, the hopelessness of the unemployed. They have, what government has not, the *power* to do this; they lack only the intelligence to grasp the situation, and the resolution to act. In face of such a state of things as this, has the propagandist of Socialism, who will none of parliamentary elections, no sphere of action left but homicide? Such a question, we say again, is absurd, and we only raise and answer it here because certain Social Democrats have now and again considered it worth asking.

III. – While homicidal outrages are neither a logical outcome of Anarchist principles nor a practical necessity of Anarchist action, they are a social phenomenon which Anarchists and all Social Revolutionists must be prepared to face.
There is a truism that the man in the street seems always to forget, when he is abusing the Anarchists, or whatever party happens to be his *bête noir* for the moment, as the cause of some outrage just perpetrated. This indisputable fact is that homicidal outrages have, from time immemorial, been the reply of goaded and desperate classes, and goaded and desperate individuals, to wrongs from their fellow men which they felt to be intolerable. Such acts are the violent recoil from violence, whether aggressive or repressive; they are the last desperate struggle of outraged and exasperated human nature for breathing space and life. And their cause lies not in any special conviction, but in the depths of that human nature itself. The whole course of history, political and social, is strewn with evidence of this fact. To go no further, take the three most notorious examples of political parties goaded into outrage during the last thirty years: the Mazzinians in Italy, the Fenians in Ireland, and the Terrorists in Russia. Were these people Anarchists? No. Did they all three even hold the same political opinions? No. The Mazzinians were Republicans, the Fenians political separatists, the Russians Social Democrats or Constitutionalists. But all were driven by desperate circumstances into this terrible form of revolt. And when we turn from parties to individuals

who have acted in like manner, we stand appalled by the number of human beings goaded and driven by sheer desperation into conduct obviously violently opposed to their social instincts.

Now that Anarchism has become a living force in society, such deeds have been sometimes committed by Anarchists, as well as by others. For no new faith, even the most essentially peaceable and humane the mind of man has as yet accepted, but at its first coming has brought upon earth not peace but a sword; not because of anything violent or anti-social in the doctrine itself; simply because of the ferment any new and creative idea excites in men's minds, whether they accept or reject it. And a conception like Anarchism, which, on the one hand, threatens every vested interest, and, on the other, holds out a vision of a free and noble life to be won by struggle against existing wrongs, is certain to rouse the fiercest opposition, and bring the whole repressive force of ancient evil into violent contact with the tumultuous outburst of a new hope.

Under miserable conditions of life, any vision of the possibility of better things makes the present misery more intolerable, and spurs those who suffer to the most energetic struggles to improve their lot, and if these struggles only immediately result in sharper misery, the outcome is often sheer desperation. In our present society, for instance, an exploited wage-worker, who catches a glimpse of what work and life might and ought to be, finds the toilsome routine, and the squalor of his existence almost intolerable; and even when he has the resolution and courage to continue steadily working his best, and waiting till the new ideas have so permeated society as to pave the way for better times, the mere fact that he has such ideas, and tries to spread them, brings him into difficulties with his employers. How many thousands of Socialists, and above all of Anarchists have lost work, and even the chance of work, solely on the ground of their opinions. It is only the specially gifted craftsman who, if he be a zealous propagandist, can hope to retain permanent employment. And what happens to a man with his brains working actively with a ferment of new ideas, with a vision before his eyes of a new hope dawning for toiling and agonising men, with the knowledge that his suffering and that of his fellows in misery is caused not by the cruelty of Fate but by the injustice of other human beings, – what happens to such a man when he sees those dear to him starving, when he himself is starved? Some natures in such a plight, and those by no means the least social or the least sensitive, will become violent, and will even feel that their violence is social and not anti-social, that in striking when and how they can, they are striking not for themselves but for human nature, outraged and despoiled in their persons and in those of their fellow sufferers. And are we, who ourselves are not in this horrible predicament, to stand by and coldly condemn these piteous victims of the Furies and the Fates? Are we to decry as miscreants these human beings, who act often with heroic self-devotion, sacrificing their lives in protest where less social and energetic natures would lie down and grovel in abject submission to injustice and wrong? Are we to join the ignorant and brutal outcry which stigmatises such men as monsters of wickedness, gratuitously running amuck in a harmonious and innocently peaceful society? No! We hate murder with a hatred that may seem absurdly exaggerated to apologists for Matabele massacres, to callous acquiescers in hangings and bombardments, but we decline, in such cases of homicide or attempted homicide as those of which we are treating, to be guilty of the cruel injustice of flinging the whole responsibility of the deed upon the immediate perpetrator. The guilt of these homicides lies upon every man and woman who, intentionally or by cold indifference, helps to keep up social conditions that drive human beings to despair. The man who flings his whole soul into the attempt, at the cost of his own life, to protest against the wrongs of his fellow men, is a saint compared to the active and passive upholders of cruelty and injustice, even if his protest destroy other lives besides his own. Let him who is without sin in society cast the first stone at such an one.

But we say to no man: "Go AND DO THOU LIKEWISE." The man who in ordinary circumstances and in cold blood would commit such deeds is simply a homicidal maniac; nor do we believe they can be justified upon any mere ground of expediency. Least of all do we think that any human being has a right to egg on another person to such a course of action. We accept the phenomena of homicidal outrage as among the most terrible facts of human experience; we endeavour to look such facts full in the face with the understanding of humane justice; and we believe that we are doing our utmost to put an end to them by spreading Anarchist ideas throughout society.

Suppose a street where the drainage system has got thoroughly out of order, and the foulness of the sewer gas is causing serious illness throughout the neighbourhood. The intelligent inhabitants will first of all seek the cause of the illness, and then, having traced it to the condition of the drainage, will insist upon laying the sewer open, investigating the state of the pipes, and where needful, laying new ones. In this process it is very probable indeed that the illness in the neighbourhood may be temporarily increased by the laying open of the foulness within, and that some of those who do the work may be themselves poisoned, or carry the infection to others. But is that a reason for not opening and repairing the drain? Or would it be fair or rational to say the illness in the neighbourhood was caused by the people who did this work or insisted upon it being done? Yet such is much the attitude of those critics of Anarchism who try to make it appear that we Anarchists are responsible for what is the natural result of the social evils we point out and struggle against.

And how about those Anarchists who use bloodthirsty language? No words can be too strong to denounce the wrongs now inflicted by one human being upon another; but violent language is by no means the same as forcible language, and very often conveys an impression of weakness rather than of strength. Savage talk is often a sort of relief, which half desperate men give to their tortured nerves; sometimes it is the passionate expression of the frenzy of indignation felt by an enthusiastically social nature at the sight of oppression and suffering: or it may be only the harebrained rattle of a fool seeking a sensation; but whatever its nature, our position with regard to it is well expressed by Mr Auberon Herbert in his letter to the *Westminster Gazette*, Nov. 22 [1893]: "Of all the miserable, unprofitable, inglorious wars in the world is the war against words. Let men say just what they like. Let them propose to cut every throat and burn every house – if so they like it. We have nothing to do with a man's words or a man's thoughts, except to put against them better words or better thoughts, and so to win in the great moral and intellectual duel that is always going on, and on which all progress depends."

Every man, Anarchist or not, must speak as he thinks fit, but if an Anarchist cannot resist using the language of bloodthirsty revenge, he would do very well to follow the honest example recently set by the editor of the *Commonweal*, and plainly say, "This is not Anarchism."

                    [*Freedom*, Volume 7, Number 83, December 1893]

A Brief History of Freedom

{Fourteen years ago – that is to say, in October, 1886 – the first number of} *Freedom* {appeared. It} was started in October 1886, by Peter Kropotkine & C.M. Wilson, the latter acting as Editor. [Its principles as laid down in the first no. were Communist-Anarchism. Amongst its contributors, during the first year of its existence, were Edward Carpenter, Dr Burns-Gibson, G. Bernard Shaw, H. Havelock Ellis, Sydney Olivier, Dr Merlino, E. Prowse Reilly, N.F. Dryhurst, & Henry Glasse.] It was a small double sheet, containing a leader on some current topic, notes on passing events, one or two short theoretical or literary articles, a poem sometimes, & a monthly chronicle of "The Struggle for Freedom" in the world. In this form the paper appeared monthly for two years & a quarter.

In the autumn of 1887, the Anarchist movement in England, as elsewhere, received a noteworthy impetus from the storm of indignation raised amongst the workers by the infamous condemnation of the Chicago strike leaders, five of whom were, on the strength of their Anarchist opinions, hanged on a false charge of bomb throwing. *Freedom* took a leading part in getting up indignation meetings in London, working for that purpose with the Socialist League & Social Democratic Federation. In consequence, the paper was obliged, in deference to the strongly anti-Anarchist views of Mr Bradlaugh, to remove from its original office in the premises of the Free Thought Publishing Company, in Bouverie St., where it had its headquarters through the kindness of Mrs Besant. It found temporary office room with the good-hearted Editor of the *Leaflet Newspaper*, T. Bolas, in Cursitor Street, until, in July 1888, T. Binning, at the Labor Union Printery, afterwards the Labor Press, undertook its publication. From its first appearance until that date, *Freedom* was set up at the Socialist League printing office, by the kind permission of William Morris.

During the first year of the paper's existence a small group of propagandists, began gradually to gather about it, with the object of pushing its sale & spreading the idea it represented. Early in 1888, they obtained the loan of the Socialist League Hall in Farringdon St. for a series of public discussion meetings. The first took place Feb. 16, & the meetings were continued monthly for the remainder of the year, with very useful results in developing & making known Anarchist ideas.

[A considerable influence was exercised upon the English movement, in the autumn of this same year, by the visit of Mrs Parsons, widow of one of the Anarchists hanged at Chicago. She addressed numerous meetings, arousing much sympathy amongst the workers, both for the cause & for the Chicago men, but choking off various lukewarm or partial sympathisers with Anarchist theories by her "Wild West" talk about fighting.]

[About this time the ranks of the contributors to *Freedom* were re-inforced by A. Marsh, J. Blackwell, Edith Nesbit (Mrs Bland), Dr Lazarus ("Edgeworth"), J.M. Fells, O. Bertoni, Dyer Lum & T. Pearson.]

In the early part of 1889, C.M. Wilson leaving London for a time, J. Blackwell became joint-editor & the group, drawing its organisation closer, began to take active part in the management of the paper, which re-appeared, after two months' suspension, in March 1889. The International Chronicle was now dropped & occasional articles from foreign correspondents substituted. A serial running on from month to month was also started, the first being "The Revolt of the English Workers in the XIX Century" by C.M. Wilson. The plan answered & the first serial was followed by Jean Grave's "Morrow of the Revolution" & several essays by P. Kropotkine & E. Malatesta, since republished as pamphlets.

In August, 1889, some type was bought & a single sheet supplement, set up by volunteers, issued with the paper. In September a chronicle of the propaganda in London was begun. This was the germ of the regular reports & notices of the English Anarchist movement which have since become a feature of *Freedom* & the steady growth of Anarchist ideas may be excellently studied in the increasing space devoted year by year to the reports & notices of groups all over the country.

In April 1890 a fresh series of discussion meetings was started by the *Freedom* Group, held in the Autonomie Hall, by kind permission of the Club, & continued weekly until the close of May. In the summer of this year, reports from provincial groups began to be sent regularly to *Freedom*. In November, the *Freedom* Group organised a large public meeting at South Place, & as well as several smaller local gatherings, to commemorate the legal murder of the Chicago Anarchists. It proved a great success & a public meeting on similar lines has been held each succeeding year. The Group also organised a special Commemoration of the Paris Commune in the following March, instead of sending its speakers to the meeting organised by the Social Democrats. This also was very successful & was for several years successfully repeated.

[Amongst the new contributors to the paper at this time were A. Tarn, Charles Malato, E. Malatesta, J. Bruce Glasier, Arne Dybfish, John Marshall, J.G. Barlas, C. Porter, C. Morton, H. Davis, Dr Netlow, E.L. Voynich, J. Andrews (Australia) & S. Mella (Spain).]

In Jan. 1891, *Freedom* again removed, & took up its quarters with the New Fellowship Press, Newington Green, where it had its own office and type under the management of W. Wess but was published by the N.F. Press. In February the single sheet supplement was given up and the size of the paper permanently doubled. At this time, J. Blackwell resigned the co-editorship, leaving C.M. Wilson again alone as editor.

In March, 1891 an Anarchist Conference was held to consider the policy of English Anarchists with regard to the May Labor Demonstration. The *Freedom* Group organised a social gathering to bring the country & London delegates into touch the evening before the Conference, which was a great success & the first of many arranged for special purposes of this sort. The Conference decided that Anarchists might with great profit make use of the proposed demonstration, whenever held, as a means of propaganda; but that any demonstration organised by them should take place on *May First*, that being the day claimed by the workers as their holiday, specially to be devoted to the celebration of the solidarity of Labor & the voicing of its claims; a principle which has been upheld by Anarchists year after year. The first May Day meetings had been held in 1890, Anarchists & Social Democrats informally taking part together in London & the Hyde Park meeting had been very enthusiastic. The separate Anarchist meeting in 1891, on the First, was enthusiastic but small; the Social Democratic gathering, on May 3rd., large but dull, the demand for the legal eight hours failing to rouse much enthusiasm. During the summer much energetic propaganda was done by small meetings in the Parks. In Regents Park a regular peripatetic school of Anarchist philosophy was formed, the same audience assembling week after week, summer after summer, to discuss & dispute with F. Hyde and other comrades.

With 1892 began an era of repression on the one hand & revolt on the other throughout the civilised world. In England, first came the Walsall Police Plot; exposed, month by month, as it dragged out its shameful details before the courts by *Freedom*, which also opened a defence fund for the prisoners. Next followed the prosecution of the *Commonweal* for taking the same line in less measured English. Meanwhile unemployed riots in Germany & the Ravachol affair in France were followed by great strikes in Australia, in the English shipping, weaving & coal trades, the Carnegie riots & violent police persecutions in America, colliers' riots in Belgium, riotous strikes in Bristol, Hull, Austria, Italy; then came the great English coal war, the Sicilian revolt; then the Barcelona, Vaillant, Bourdin, Henri, Carnot, Roman affairs, all, or almost all, met or provoked by the violence of governments; strikes put down by armed force, prosecutions for opinions and "tendencies", savage sentences; wholesale press prosecutions in Germany, anti-Anarchist laws in France, the trials of Grave & the Thirty; endless imprisonments & several barbarous executions in Italy & Spain; an era of violence & wholesale injustice.

In England during the same period we had the François & Meunier extraditions, the Cantwell & Young & Cantwell & Quinn prosecutions & the attacks on Free Speech, notably in Hyde Park & at Manchester. During this troublous two years, *Freedom* stood firmly on the side of the rebels & against the suppression of rebellion in word & deed, even when the rebels used weapons which no humane person can approve in cold blood. (See "Anarchism & Outrage", republished from *Freedom* for Dec. 1893. "Desperate men cannot choose their methods, if those methods are brutal & revolting, the crime lies mainly with those men who drive their fellows to desperation.") On the other hand *Freedom* did not either advocate or applaud outrage; its own policy advocated a continuous & energetic endeavour on the part of the workers, organised in Trades Unions, Cooperative Societies & other voluntary associations, to obtain by direct action, such as refusing to work as wage-slaves, the control of the means of production; so that the producers & distributors may become their own employers, with the right to dispose of what they make.

[In Oct. 1892 *Freedom* was once more compelled to remove & took up its quarters with Mr & Mrs Hyde, who had for years taken an active part in the business of its distribution. In Feb. 1893 it removed with them from Kentish Town to Miss Henry's house in St. Augustine's Road, the office manager, W. Wess, removing there also, with the type. During the winter of 1892-3 & again from Sept. - Dec. 1894 C.M. Wilson was called away by illness in her family & the editorship was temporarily taken by N.F. Dryhurst, who for some time sub-edited the propaganda column.]

In July 1892, an appeal, written by W. Wess, and first published in *Freedom*, was issued as a leaflet by some Anarchist trades-unionists, calling upon British Trade Societies to insist upon fair play for Anarchist Labor Delegates at the Zurich Congress. The manifest unfairness with which all anti-Parliamentarian debates, unpleasing to the Marxist leaders, were treated on that occasion called forth much indignation, & found expression in *Freedom* in a series of able anti-Marxist articles by W. Tcherkazov, an old Internationalist. [Other new contributors about this time were W. Wess, Cyril Bell, Ernest Radford, G. Naewiger, E. Malatesta, Ignaz Sheppard, H. Duncan, J. Sketchley, W.C. Owen, A. Henry, Dr Macdonald, G. Lawrence, U. Rosselli, J. A. Brown, Louise Bevington, Louise Michel, C. Kenworthy, G. Steffen & H. Nevinson.]

In Jan. 1895, C.M. Wilson was obliged, by family reasons, to conclude her eight years & four months' editorship of *Freedom* and the paper was suspended for three months until new arrangements could be made. In May, it reappeared under the editorship of A. Marsh & J. Turner & T. Cantwell, the two latter who had been for many years connected with *The Commonweal*, joining *Freedom* when their own paper fell through.

{Since that time *Freedom* has continued to appear as regularly as circumstances would allow, although the reaction which has blighted so many advanced movements has not decreased the difficulties that always beset the publication of an Anarchist journal. But as the printing of the whole series of the paper, and as these amount in the aggregate to over 80,000, it may surely be said that enough has been accomplished to warrant us in continuing our efforts and even in redoubling them. We hope this brief statement will induce comrades and sympathisers to take the same view and give us what help is in their power.}

[Manuscript, International Institute of Social History, September 1896; *Freedom*, Volume 14, Number 154, December 1900]

Notes

Anarchism (1884)

This was based on a lecture to the Fabian Society; according to the Society Minutes for 7 November 1884, "Mrs Wilson read a paper on Anarchism. A discussion followed." *Justice* was from January 1884 the monthly paper of the Democratic Federation, which was formed by the Radical politician Henry Mayers Hyndman in June 1881, and which adopted a Socialist programme and adopted the name Social Democratic Federation in August 1884; in December 1884 it split between supporters and opponents of Hyndman, the latter forming the Socialist League. It was edited by Hyndman himself, and generally followed a fairly strict Marxist line.

In Lyon sixty-eight anarchists were prosecuted (fourteen in their absence) for membership of and involvement in the International Working-Men's Association, following a series of strikes and attacks during 1882. Their trial was held from 8 to 19 January 1883 and their appeal from 26 February to 6 March, and the proceedings were reported in the *Gazette des tribunaux* and then in a book – *Le procès des anarchistes devant la Police correctionnelle et la Cour d'appel de Lyon* (1883). On Friday afternoon, 12 January, Félix Tressaud, one of the accused, read "with a firm voice and with conviction" a "Declaration of the Anarchists accused before the Correctional Tribunal of Lyon". It was stated to have been signed by forty-seven of them (actually forty-six, Victor Berlioz-Arthaud being counted as two people), and to have been drafted by one of them, Peter Kropotkin, who was the best-known defendant and one of the four who were sentenced to five years' imprisonment. The Declaration was widely publicised in the national and international press, and it was published in full in the special double issue of the leading French anarchist paper *Le Révolté* (20 January / 3 February 1883) and later in the *Procès des anarchistes* (pages 66-68). A translation of it in a leaflet published in London on 23 January 1883 by the International Socialist Federation as *Manifesto of the Socialists tried in Lyon by the French Republican Government* was one of the first explicitly anarchist texts published in English. It was later republished in *The Republican* (April 1884) and in the first issue of *The Anarchist* (March 1885).

Pierre Joseph Proudhon proclaimed, "Property is theft", at the beginning of his book *Qu'est-ce que la propriété?* (What is Property?) in 1840; later in the same book he was the first person to call himself an "anarchist". Henri de

Saint-Simon, the pioneering French socialist, did not in fact lay down a formula for his theory, but after his death his followers did so, though it was not as quoted by Charlotte Wilson. Their ideas were expounded in a series of public meetings given in Paris in 1828-1829 and immediately reported first in their papers and then in a series of books. At the meeting on 25 February 1829, recorded in *Doctrine de Saint-Simon: Exposition, Premier année 1829* (1830), Saint-Amand Bazard stated: *"To each according to his capacity, to each capacity according to his work."* This meant that each person would be allotted a position in society according to his aptitudes, and would be rewarded according to his work in that position; this was later modified into the simpler version, *From each according to his capacity, to each according to his work.* It was not the Socialists led by the Saint-Simonians but the Communists led by Etienne Cabet who coined the amended version, *From each following his faculty, to each following his needs*, which was first printed on the title-page of the third edition of his utopian novel *Voyage à l'Icarie* (Voyage to Icaria) in 1845. This was adopted by the moderate Socialist leader Louis Blanc during the 1848 Revolution, and was afterwards used by both Socialists and Communists (including Karl Marx), and also by Anarchist Collectivists and Communists.

Arnold Toynbee was a short-lived idealistic philanthropist in late Victorian England, whose lectures to working people in East London were published posthumously as *Industrial Revolution* (1884); Toynbee Hall was founded in his memory. Herbert Spencer, as well as being the main exponent of a naturalistic and evolutionist view of the world in Victorian Britain, was also the main exponent of extreme Liberalism in politics, from *The Proper Sphere of Government* (1843) to *The Man versus the State* (1885). His ideology, opposing both the welfare state and the warfare state, foreshadowed what was later called Libertarianism. The chapter on "The Right to Ignore the State", which was included in the first edition but omitted from later editions of his book *Social Statics: or, The Conditions Essential to Human Happines Specified ...* (1851), was after his death half a century later reprinted as an Anarchist pamphlet on both sides of the Atlantic and in several languages. His book *Education: Intellectual, Moral, and Physical* (1861), based on articles published between 1854 and 1859, was very influential and was frequently reprinted and translated for more than half a century. Michael Bakunin's fragment known as *God and the State* was written in 1871 and posthumously published in 1882; an English translation produced by Benjamin Tucker in the United States in 1883 was circulated in Britain by Henry Seymour, and another by Marie Le Compte was serialised by Henry Seymour in *The Anarchist* during 1885.

The quotation from Walt Whitman comes from the opening paragraph of his main prose work, *Democratic Vistas* (1871). Giuseppe Mazzini, the intellectual leader of the *Risorgimento*, the struggle for an independent and united republic in Italy, spent thirty years in exile in England; he repeatedly emphasised the importance of moral as well as political progress, including the conscious development of brotherhood.

A long reply to Charlotte Wilson's articles by "An English Socialist" was published with the title "Collectivism", expressing "a plain and straightforward statement of the collectivist or social-democratic view" (what we would call State socialism), and dismissing anarchism as ineffective individualism (*Justice*, 20 December 1884).

Justice (1885)

The Latin motto means "Light in the darkness; hope in the light". The story of the reformed thief Jean Valjean is told in Victor Hugo's long novel *Les Misérables*, written from 1845 to 1861 and published in ten volumes in 1862, and the attack on capital punishment in his short story *Le Dernier jour d'un condamné*, written in 1828 and published in 1829; the 1832 edition of the latter contained a long preface giving a detailed explanation of Hugo's arguments against capital punishment. Francis Bacon's essay "Of Revenge" begins: "Revenge is a kinde of Wilde Justice; which the more Mans Nature runs to, the more ought Law to weed it out" (*Essayes, or Counsels Civill and Morall*, 1625). Bacon, as a lawyer, a member of both Houses of Parliament for nearly forty years, and holder of several offices culminating in that of Lord Chancellor, was naturally in favour of the law, until he was impeached for bribery and removed from all his positions in 1621. Charlotte Wilson's argument anticipates that of Peter Kropotkin's essay *L'Organisation de la vindicte appelée justice* (1900), translated into English as *Organised Vengeance Called Justice* (1901).

The Criminal Law Amendment Act (1885)

The Criminal Law Amendment Bill, which was intended to reduce child prostitution by raising the age of consent by females to sexual intercourse from thirteen to sixteen and by penalising those who controlled prostitutes or procured females for immoral purposes, was first introduced by the Liberal government in 1883, but it was skilfully obstructed, and it seemed to be doomed by the election of a Conservative government in 1885.

However, prompted by a coalition of religious interests, William Thomas Stead, a practitioner of the so-called "new journalism" and editor from 1883 to 1889 of the *Pall Mall Gazette*, a sensational Liberal evening paper, started a violent campaign against child prostitution with a series of scandalous articles called "The Maiden Tribute of Modern Babylon", published from 6 July to 12 July 1885 and immediately reprinted as a pamphlet. Charlotte Wilson supported a resolution of the Fabian Society congratulating the paper on 18 July. The effect on public opinion was so overwhelming that the Bill was passed on 10 August and became law on 14 August 1885. (At a late stage, on 6 August, Henry Labouchère introduced an amendment to the Bill adding the criminal offence of "gross indecency" between males in private, which led to the downfall of Oscar Wilde in 1895 and lasted until 1967.) Stead continued to play an active part in the campaign, and took the leading place in a huge demonstration in Hyde Park on 22 August. However, in purchasing a girl of thirteen to demonstrate the weakness of the existing law, he had actually broken it, and he was successfully prosecuted and in November 1885 sentenced to three months' imprisonment.

John Milton wrote *Areopagitica* (1644) in defence of the right of publication without prior licence by the Stationers' Company. He later worked for the Commonwealth and Protectorate (1649-1660), which tried to operate its own censorship. The Babylonian king Nebuchadnezzar, who persecuted the Jews after conquering Judaea, is said to have eaten grass during his bout of madness described in the Biblical book of Daniel.

The Contagious Diseases Acts from 1864 to 1869, which were intended to reduce venereal disease in the armed services by regulating prostitutes in eighteen garrison and sea-port towns, involved the compulsory medical examination of women suspected of being prostitutes, and were eventually repealed after a similar public campaign in 1886.

Michael Davitt (1846-1906) was a leading Irish Nationalist all his adult life, especially important as a link between the militant and moderate wings, between the agrarian and political agitations, and between the British and American movements. He was prosecuted for treason-felony in 1870, and sentenced to fifteen years' penal servitude. He was imprisoned for seven years until he was released on ticket-of-leave, and he was later imprisoned for sedition in 1879-1880, in 1881-1882, and in 1883. He described his experiences of prison and his observations of criminals in a pamphlet, *The Prison Life of Michael Davitt* (1878), and in a book, *Leaves from a Prison Diary* (1884); a section of the latter was published as an article on "The Punishment of Penal Servitude" in the *Contemporary Review* (August 1883), which made a considerable impact. He was far from being an anarchist, but he was a strong opponent of imprisonment as an answer to crime, recommending the spread of education and the elimination of poverty as the most effective methods. He was elected to Parliament several times from 1892 to 1895 and he sat from 1895 to 1899. He was a Socialist and Secularist as well as a Nationalist and Republican.

The Club alluded to was the Men and Women's Club.

Charlotte Wilson contributed an article with the title "Criminal Law Amendment" to *The Anarchist* in August 1885, and a revised and expanded version was immediately published as a pamphlet with the addition of an appendix and with the title *The Criminal Law Amendment Act*, in both cases under the same pseudonym. The latter is the text used here.

Social Democracy and Anarchism (1886)

The Practical Socialist, described as "A Monthly Review of Evolutionary or Non-revolutionary Socialism", was the short-lived paper of the Fabian Society during 1886, edited by Thomas Bolas. Charlotte Wilson explained in a letter to Karl Pearson (7 February 1886) that this "was not an article, but the summary of a lecture"; and she added that "I do consider Anarchism the one living, growing faith".

What Socialism Is (1886)

This was the fourth tract published by the Fabian Society, designed to explain the two main forms of Socialism to English readers. An editorial note announced: "The following tract has been prepared by certain members of the Fabian Society with the view of supplying information as to the opinions largely held throughout the world by those who call themselves Socialists; but it must not be assumed that these opinions are endorsed by the Fabian Society collectively, or necessarily by any member of it."

The stages of its preparation in late 1885 and early 1886 may be traced in the minutes of the Fabian Society (in the Fabian Society Papers held at the London School of Economics & Political Science). It was always assumed that Charlotte Wilson would write the section on Anarchism. The Executive Committee decided in December 1885 and January 1886 that Friedrich Engels should be asked to write the section on Collectivism, in January 1886 that if he didn't agree she should be asked to do so, and in February 1886 that her draft should be accepted. At this point Bernard Shaw wrote to Hubert Bland that "Mrs Wilson's tract on collectivism, as I from the first foresaw, seems certain now to end in a ruin. I think we must either withdraw or allow Mrs Bl. [Edith Nesbit] to take it in hand" (letter, 8 February 1886); but clearly they were overruled. Charlotte Wilson and Edward Pease had written separate drafts of the Introduction; the Executive Committee decided in December 1885 that Sidney Webb should choose between them, and in January 1886 his choice of her draft was accepted. The Society decided in February 1886 that the planned pamphlet should be accepted, but that a special Executive Committee should consider and amend the introduction; this was done in March 1886, and the Society accepted the result in April 1886. The pamphlet was published in June 1886. Its epigraph was a quotation from Francis Bacon's essay *Of Innovations*:

> As the Births of Living Creatures, at first, are ill shapen: So are all *Innovations*, which are the Births of Time ... Time is the greatest *Innovatour*: And if Time, of course, alter Things to the worse, and Wisedome, and Counsell shall not alter them to the better, what shall be the End?

August Bebel was a leading member of the Sozialdemokratische Partei Deutschlands (Social-democratic Party of Germany) and a prolific writer. His book *Die Frau in der Vergangenheit, Gegenwart und Zukunft* (1883) was translated into English by H.B.A. Walther as *Woman in Past, Present and Future* (1885).

The quotation from the American Transcendentalist writer Ralph Waldo Emerson, from "Self-Reliance" in his first series of *Essays* (1841), a key text of individualism, continues as follows:

> Society everywhere is in conspiracy against the manhood of every one of its members. Society is a joint-stock company, in which the members agree, for the better securing of his bread to each shareholder, to surrender the liberty and culture of the eater. The virtue in most request is conformity. Self-reliance is its aversion. It loves not realities and creators, but names and customs. Whoso would be a man must be a nonconformist. He who would gather immortal palms must not be hindered by the name of goodness, but must explore if it be goodness. Nothing is at last sacred but the integrity of your own mind ...

The phrase "direct personal action" in the penultimate sentence anticipates the phrase direct action, the key concept of the later anarcho-syndicalist movement.

Despite Shaw's general hostility to Anarchism and specific disagreements with Charlotte Wilson, remained friendly with her and contributed material to *Freedom* from the start, as noted in his Diary (12 September 1886, 20 April 1887, 10 October 1887).

The Principles and Aims of Anarchists (1886)

The Present Day, described variously as "A Monthly Review of Politics, Sociology, Laws, Philosophy, Dialectics, Morals and Literature" or as "Short Essays on Social, Economic and Ethical Subjects", was the last of G.J. Holyoake's many Secularist periodicals, which he began in 1883 and handed over in May 1886 to Thomas Squire Barrett, the honorary secretary of the London Dialectical Society, who produced four more issues before it closed. The London Dialectical Society was a debating society formed in imitation of the more prestigious Metaphysical Society.

Freedom (1886)

This was the anonymous leading article in the first issue of *Freedom*, dated October 1886 but available at the meeting at Anderton's Hotel on 17 September 1886. It was subtitled "A Journal of Anarchist Socialism", later amended to "A Journal of Anarchism Communism".

Work (1888)

This was the text of the talk which Charlotte Wilson gave to the Freedom Group Discussion Meeting on June 1888 and which was published in *Freedom* the following month. By an oversight Thomas Keell included it in the list of anonymous articles contributed by Peter Kropotkin to the first issues of *Freedom* which he supplied to Max Nettlau in 1932, although the announcement of the meeting in *Freedom* (June 1888) stated that "C. M. Wilson will read a paper on, Work and the Distribution of Wealth", and the report of the meeting in *Freedom* (July 1888) stated that "the subject was opened last month by C.M. Wilson, who dwelt upon work as a spontaneous and voluntary expression of human energy. The substance of her paper will be found in another column." As a result, it is mistakenly attributed to Kropotkin in the relevant volume of Nettlau's *Geschichte der Anarchie – Die erste Blütezeit der Anarchie: 1886-1894* (1981).

The first paragraph is based on quotations from the Bible – first God's curse on Adam for eating the fruit of the knowledge of good and evil (Genesis 3);

then the Preacher's statement that "much study is a weariness of the flesh" (Ecclesiastes 12). G. F. Watts was a fashionable painter in 19th-century Britain. The Vestry was the 19th-century form of a local authority.

Democracy or Anarchism (1890)

This article was anonymous, but in the marked set of *Freedom* in the British Library of Political & Economic Science it is signed 'C.M.W.' in Charlotte Wilson's handwriting. It may well have been the text of the talk with which she began the first Freedom Group Discussion Meeting on 16 February 1888 and which was reported in *Freedom* (March 1888) as follows:

> The opening paper (read by C.M. Wilson) dwelt upon the necessity for Socialists to consider the political side of social re-organisation. If the revolutionists are not prepared, when the time for action comes, to introduce new political relations corresponding to the new economic relations they desire to establish, the social revolution may well be seriously delayed by the reactionary tendencies of prejudiced or ambitious politicians. The paper then briefly contrasted Democracy, i.e., representation and majority rule, with anarchism, i.e., free association, decision by unanimity and temporary delegation for definite purposes; and contended that Democracy is the political form of our transition period, and Anarchism that of true Socialism.

Walt Whitman and Edward Carpenter were respectively American and British writers who invoked a vague concept of Democracy in their free verse poems for liberty. The quotation from John Stuart Mill is not, as might be expected, from his essays *On Liberty* (1859) but from his *Principles of Political Economy* (1848), in the section on "Limits on the Province of Government" entitled "On the Grounds and Limits of the Laisser-Faire or Non-Interference Principle" (Book V, Chapter 11). The battles of the Greeks against overwhelming Persian odds at Marathon in 490 BC (as reported by Herodotus) and of the Romans against overwhelming Etruscan odds at Rome in 510 BC (as reported by Livy) were two of the Classical myths of the victory of the small over the great.

Anarchism and Homicidal Outrage (1893)

This anonymous leading article was published in response to the hostile reaction to the explosion of a bomb in the Liceo theatre in Barcelona on 7 November 1893, one of a wave of outrages perpetrated by or attributed to

Anarchist terrorists, especially in Spain and France, during the early 1890s. It was reprinted (with the omission of the line spaces and the final paragraph, probably for reasons of space) as an anonymous pamphlet with the title *Anarchism and Outrage*, published by C.M. Wilson as Freedom Pamphlet number 8 in December 1893. This was reprinted in 1909 at the time of the Tragic Week in Barcelona and the judicial murder of the anarchist educationist Francisco Ferrer y Guardia. The whole article was included in *What is Anarchism? an Introduction* (1993), edited by Donald Rooum. The present text is taken from the original version.

The quotation from Walt Whitman comes from "Salut au monde!", a section of the second edition of *Leaves of Grass* in 1856 and of the final edition in 1891, in which he salutes all the peoples of the world. Auberon Herbert was first a Conservative and then a Liberal politician, a Member of Parliament from 1870 to 1874, who became a Secularist, a Republican, a vegetarian, and what was later called a Libertarian. *The Commonweal* was from March 1885 the paper of the Socialist League; it was originally edited by William Morris, but when the Socialist League became anarchist in 1890 it was edited first by David Nicoll (who was imprisoned for his angry response to the imprisonment of Anarchists framed in the Walsall trial of 1892) and then by H. B. Samuels (who moved from militant Anarchism to virtual nihilism and later back to Marxist Socialism).

A Short History of *Freedom* (1896)

This was written after Charlotte Wilson had finally retired from *Freedom* in 1895. She explained in a covering letter to Alfred Marsh on 28 September 1896:

> Herewith my recollections as regards *Freedom*'s history for the 8 years & 4 months during which I had to do with it, as far as I can recall matters by glancing through the files. The first few years I have a note of the writer added to each article &c., not for the last four years, so during that time I may have omitted one or two new contributors, but not many I fancy … There are a great many more things I might have introduced but had not time for more researches & thought you really wanted more from me, a general sketch of the whole; you & others can add things more in detail which you remember.

(Her marked set of *Freedom* is held in the British Library of Political & Economic Science.) However, the article was published (in an abridged form) only in December 1900; by this time she seems to have forgotten it, since she wrote to Alfred Marsh on 4 January 1901: "Of course I noted with particular interest your excellent summary of the history of the paper last month." The version here is taken from the original manuscript "History of *Freedom*. Rough notes. C.M.W." (held in the International Institute of Social History, Amsterdam – the last page is missing). The passages which were excluded from the published version [indicated by square brackets] give a valuable first-hand record of early contributors to *Freedom*, including several well-known liberal intellectuals of the time (with some errors in the spelling of names). The opening and closing passages of the published version {indicated by braces} were supplied by the editor.

Freedom Press also publishes the fortnightly journal
Freedom and the *The Raven* (quarterly).
Contact us for current subscription rates and copy of our
booklist at the address below:

FREEDOM PRESS
84b Whitechapel High Street, London E1 7QX